Bank Lending to
Business Borrowers

Bank Lending to Business Borrowers

Interest Rates and U.S. Monetary Policy

Weir M. Brown

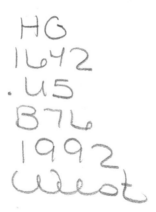

Westview Press

BOULDER • SAN FRANCISCO • OXFORD

This Westview softcover edition is printed on acid-free paper and bound in library-quality, coated covers that carry the highest rating of the National Association of State Textbook Administrators, in consultation with the Association of American Publishers and the Book Manufacturers' Institute.

Copyright © 1992 by Westview Press, Inc.

Published in 1992 in the United States of America by Westview Press, Inc., 5500 Central Avenue, Boulder, Colorado 80301-2877, and in the United Kingdom by Westview Press, 36 Lonsdale Road, Summertown, Oxford OX2 7EW

Library of Congress Cataloging-in-Publication Data
Brown, Weir M. (Weir Messick), 1914–
   Bank lending to business borrowers : interest rates and U.S.
monetary policy / by Weir M. Brown.
      p.   cm.
   Includes bibliographical references.
   ISBN 0-8133-8370-6
   1. Commercial loans—United States.   2. Interest rates—United
States.   3. Monetary policy—United States.   I. Title.
HG1642.U5B76   1992
332.7'53'0973—dc20   92-32779
                                                                          CIP

Printed and bound in the United States of America

The paper used in this publication meets the requirements
of the American National Standard for Permanence of Paper
for Printed Library Materials Z39.48-1984.

10   9   8   7   6   5   4   3   2   1

In admiration of Arthur M. Okun,
who envisioned, and began to build,
"a sturdy micro-macro bridge"

Contents

Tables and Figures

Preface

Soon after embarking on the research for this book, I was able to grasp more fully how little professional attention had been devoted to serious study of short-term bank lending. Nineteenth- and twentieth-century economists had made exhaustive studies leading to systematic bodies of theory dealing with the process of capital formation financed by the issuance of long-term bonds sold at auction. By contrast, the equally active and voluminous—but different—short-term lending by banks to business firms had been either ignored by professional economists or dismissed, as transitory and inconsequential, without systematic empirical and theoretic analysis. This discrepancy seemed anomalous, in view of the importance to commercial and industrial firms of this working capital provided by banks and in view of the sensitivity of short-term loan terms to forces operating in the money markets.

Although the scanty nature of previous work in this sector prepares a rather fragmentary foundation to build upon, it whetted my curiosity, and it also indicated the necessary lines I needed to follow in attempting a modest contribution to extending the field. These lines involved finding an explanation for the preoccupation of most economic writers, whether of Keynesian or the neoclassical school of thought, with long-term financing and the bond rate; identifying, in the works of a few explorers, the elements that might contribute to a more fruitful approach to the chosen subject; and seeking to combine some of these fragments with a few of my own in pursuit of an explanation of short-term interest rates that might be somewhat more congruent with the actual behavior of the economic agents, institutions, and social environment of the "real world" than previously available.

Once it becomes fairly clear that the magnitude and behavior of short-term borrowing and lending constitute a factor of significance to the macroeconomic functioning of the system, the focus of study is increasingly centered on rates of interest. It seems pertinent to distinguish, in contemporary economic thought, two parallel and mutually reinforcing approaches to the subject, one that addresses primarily the *determination* or setting of the rate on a given new commercial and industrial loan, and the other directed more to discerning the processes or forces that influence the evolution or movement of these short-term rates.

The discussion of interest has one of the longest histories in economic literature. Anyone examining that historiography, even in a cursory fashion, must be amused or mystified by the diverse images or reactions that the topic has inspired. Medieval scholars followed the view of the Greek philosophers, who held that money was introduced to be used in exchange of goods but not to generate interest; and the Church branded interest-taking as a sin. Some nineteenth-century political economists firmly held the concept that a "natural" rate of interest (for the bond market) existed but acknowledged that it was not measurable. For some persons, both money and interest seemed to take on, at times, a veil of mystery or the supernatural. The special characteristics of the subject even led an eminent Oxford University economist to muse, "Interest is nothing but a phenomenon of the mind, the resultant of thoughts and opinions, hopes and fears, itself only a promise, finally indeed an act, but one solely originating in the will of the parties, not a physical phenomenon at all."[1] If this were literally true, it would not be surprising if the resulting consternation had hindered the economics profession from perfecting a coherent, comprehensive, and agreed theory of interest!

In this book the time frame of reference is mainly the present, as far as institutions and practices of the banking system and the Federal Reserve System are concerned. At the same time, many of the tables and graphs present data covering long periods, frequently the forty-year span 1950 to the present. Given the nature of the subject, most of the intertemporal comparisons focus on gradual or long-term changes and contrasts rather than on short-term fluctuations. Owing to the wealth of statistical material gathered and published by the Federal Reserve on financial subjects, most of the data employed below come from that source and other official agencies. For charts that do not specify their source, the origin is given in a list following the final chapter.

At various stages I was assisted by valuable conversations with, or information supplied by, persons at the Board of Governors and the several Federal Reserve Banks. I thank them all and should mention individually Normand R.V. Bernard, Thomas F. Brady, Arturo Estrella, Dennis E. Farley, Edward R. Fry, Donald L. Kohn, Virginia L. Lewis, Mary M. McLaughlin, Ann-Marie Meulendyke, and Brian Reed.

The Brookings Institution was considerate in according me special guest privileges during the greater part of the study, thus providing an agreeable base for research and scholarly association. At successive stages I benefited from the skills of Allen Sebrell, Carolyn Hill, and at the crucial stage from Beth McKenney, who was especially helpful in executing the graphic materials. Joseph P. Fennell and Sallyjune F. Kuka offered invaluable assistance on processing problems.

I owe special appreciation to several persons who either read parts of the manuscript or exchanged views with me about issues and interpretations: Margaret M. Blair, Edward F. Denison, C. David Finch, John A. Gorman, E. Michael Laub, George L. Perry, and Walter S. Salant. Their comments were valuable in correcting, confirming, or redirecting my efforts, but they bear no responsibility for the product.

Finally, I thank my wife, Maxine Stewart Brown, and my son, Peter D.G. Brown, for their encouragement, forbearance, and interdisciplinary counsel.

Weir M. Brown

Notes

1. Harrod 1973, p. 66.

1

Introduction and Background

This book seeks to examine the nature and role within the economic system of the activity carried out by commercial banks in the United States in making loans to business firms, the volume of the lending and especially the factors governing the interest rates on the loans, and the interconnections between this financial activity and the functioning of the economy in general.

One of the principal preoccupations of any modern industrialized society is judging how well its economy is performing. Judgments on this question differ among individual observers, of course, and also among social and professional groups. One country may share certain criteria and economic objectives with another, yet the relative weights placed on these criteria are likely to vary across countries and also from one time to another. Such shifts in the composition and relative importance accorded to economic goals are observable in the United States. There are a few macroeconomic objectives, however, that are widely accepted as policy goals: those of seeking to assure a fairly steady rate of growth in the output of goods and services (i.e., national product in real terms); reasonably stable price and wage levels; high and sustainable levels of employment; and freedom from distortion in the balance of international payments. An aspiring candidate that is filing application for membership in that elect group is the protective, foresighted use of environmental resources.

Measured against that set of idealistic goals, the several components of which are at times mutually incompatible, the record of the U.S. economy during the 1970s and 1980s left much to be desired. Each of the accepted objectives was compromised or not fulfilled at one time or another, and at some junctures the failings were multiple. Although the country's gross national product grew by about 71 percent in constant dollars in the twenty years from 1970 through 1989, this was well below its growth of about 101 percent in the expansive post-war years of 1950 through 1969. In the 1970s/1980s, furthermore, the growth rate varied markedly from year to year. The increase reached 6.8 percent in real (1982 dollars) terms in 1984, but in five of the twenty years the GNP actually declined.

With regard to the objective of relative stability of prices, the performance in the 1970s and 1980s was even less satisfactory. The consumer price index (CPI) published by the Bureau of Labor Statistics of the U.S. Department of Labor and calculated on the base 1982-1984 = 100, soared from 38.8 in 1970 to 124.0 in 1989, an increase of 220 percent. In the preceding 20-year span ending in 1969, the index had climbed 52 percent. During the 70s and 80s, the CPI rose 3.0 percent or more in 19 out of the 20 years, with a high of 13.3 percent. Nine of those yearly increases were above 5 percent, and 3 above 12 percent. A broader measure of price changes in the economy, the implicit price deflator for the gross national product, registered a rise of about 201 percent, somewhat below that in prices paid by urban consumers measured by the CPI but still very substantial. According to this index reflecting the average price component embodied in the value of the GNP, 12 of the years showed price increases of 5 percent or more, including 4 years with a rise of 9 to 10 percent.

Of the factors contributing to the prolonged inflationary movement of prices and wages in this period, two require special mention. The federal budget (measured on a national-income-accounts basis) had maintained approximate balance throughout the years from 1950 until the late 1960s. After that time, the mounting effects of the Vietnam war and increased social expenditures, combined with a small recession in 1970 and a sharper one in 1974-1975, began producing yearly deficits of significant proportions. By 1975 the annual shortfalls in the budget were large enough to start the outstanding governmental debt rising as a percentage of GNP. The second development was the upward shift by the private sector in the ratio of consumption to saving. The personal saving rate declined from about eight percent of disposable personal income in the early 1970s to four-six percent during most of the 1980s. This combination of dissaving by the federal government and reduced saving by the private sector created great price pressure, in the form of a total consumption demand that was growing more rapidly than gross domestic product. The resulting discrepancy between saving in the U.S. economy and the volume of borrowing required to finance planned consumer, corporate, and governmental expenditure was driving interest rates higher in financial markets. After large and rapid vertical swings from 1969 through the mid-1970s, interest rates on Treasury bills, commercial paper, and negotiable certificates of deposit surged steeply from levels of about 5 percent in 1976-1977 to peaks of 15-16 percent in 1981. Rates on short-term loans from commercial banks to business firms peaked some 3 percentage points above that.

At the same time that both the physical content and the price component of the country's gross national product were showing prolonged but irregular upward trends, the volume of employment exhibited a roughly similar upward movement, not surprisingly. The number of workers on the payrolls at nonagricultural establishments rose by 53 percent from 1970 to 1989. An additional report on employment is provided by the Bureau of Labor Statistics monthly survey of a large sample of households, covering persons 16 years of age and over. The volume of employment of persons reported in this series increased from 1970 through 1989 by 49 percent, from 78.7 to 117.3 million.

Despite the fairly steady growth in the total number of workers employed, the numbers of persons reported by the BLS survey to be unemployed also went up during the 20-year period. The higher level of unemployment was registered not only in absolute numbers but also as a percentage of the labor force, as defined. The unemployment rate during the 70s and 80s never dropped, for any year, below 4.9 percent. In ten of the 20 years the average unemployment rate remained up in the range of 7 to 10 percent of the reported labor force.

It was, indeed, this coexistence of persistently rising prices and mounting GNP in terms of current dollars, on the one hand, combined with an erratic rate of GNP growth in real terms and the chronically high rate of unemployment on the other hand, that caused the period to be characterized as one of oft-recurring "stagflation". This latter word, while not a precisely defined or uniformly used term of the professional economists' lexicon, conveys reasonably well the concept intended: that of a situation in which, at a given period, an unusual mixture of both inflationary forces and contractionary symptoms is operating in the economy at the same time.

Inevitably, the imbalances that arose or worsened during the period in the domestic economy found their reflection in the concomitant deterioration in the external accounts of the United States. The high level of consumption and investment expenditures provoked an increase in imports from abroad, and the strongly rising trend of the price level contributed to the weakening in the merchandise-trade balance. Even in current dollars, U.S. exports leveled off during the first half of the 1980s, and the balance on current account (goods and services payments) became negative from 1981 forward. Although

U.S. interest rates in banking and other financial markets have declined from their peak levels of 1981-1982, through 1990 they remained high enough, relative to international market levels, to attract a substantial volume of foreign investment in American government and corporate short- and long-term financial instruments. The resulting amount of interest payments to foreign investors has become a significant element burdening both the budgets of government and corporate debtors and the import side of the U.S. balance of international payments. These international effects of high interest rates are, of course, additional to the primarily domestic effects that high interest rates are widely presumed to have within the American economy.

When such a large number of disequilibria and roughly-matched opposing tendencies persists and even seems to threaten to become chronic, it engages the attention of economists and policymakers in the attempt to analyze the causal factors or identify policy measures that might be effective in dealing with it. This process of analysis and prescription has been actively pursued, sometimes addressing the whole stubborn complex of unstable and contradictory forces, but more often selectively studying one or another of the variable factors whose performance is associated with the major macroeconomic objectives we have been considering above.

In discussions about achieving national economic objectives, the subject of interest rates has certainly not been overlooked, either by the economics profession or by the general public. Business firms and householders alike have been made acutely aware of the keen interest-rate competition among financial institutions for their deposits or certificate accounts. Home-buyers have become expert in comparing fixed-rate mortgages with various forms of adjustable rates, along with "points" and other types of quasi-interest costs. The ability of Federal Reserve authorities to affect the federal funds rate, and thereby the volume of reserves of the banking system, by means of purchases or sales of government securities has been elucidated and closely reported in the financial press. At a more scholarly level, economists have analyzed the role of interest rates in the conduct of monetary policy; e.g., monetary aggregates *versus* the federal funds rate as the "target" for short-run monetary control operations; nominal GNP vs. real GNP (dollar volume adjusted by an interest-rate index) as the target for longer-range Fed policy; and the effect that paying an explicit interest on a given type of deposit liability may have on its volume and on its role as "money" in the technical sense. The former practice of official controls over the rates that banks pay on deposits and the effects that such rate ceilings exerted on the credit markets have been exhaustively chronicled.

Relatively little systematic examination has been given, however, to the *lending* rates of the commercial banking system. Certain other items pertaining to the asset (or income) side of the banks' financial statements have indeed been studied, such as the volume of bank loans outstanding as compared with commercial paper, or the case for and against allowing commercial banks to handle the issuance of corporate securities. By contrast, the pricing of bank loans and the movements of these prices (rates) in relation to other macroeconomic variables have received comparatively minor attention outside the Federal Reserve System. This, despite the fact that lending operations constitute one of the two halves of the basic functional role performed by the banks as intermediaries in the financial system.

In the chapters that follow, this book will seek to examine interest rates on bank loans to business firms more thoroughly both within the context of the financial sector and in relation to the functioning of the economy as a whole. In the process, it will trace the level of rates on business loans over the last forty years; compare the trends in loan rates to the evolution of other interest rates in the economy, including those of other competitive institutions; and observe the movements of the banks' lending rates in relation to their borrowing rates on deposits. Some little-used data now available from banks on how they price their business loans of different categories will be analyzed, for internal consistency as well as comparison with certain theories of interest-rate determination. In addition, consideration will be directed to the extent possible to the theoretical and empirical connection between growth rates and general price-level movements, on the one hand, and the movements of interest rates, on the other.

2

Bank Lending to Business: Basic Dimensions

This chapter gives an initial description and definition of the banking territory to be explored, and indicates the reasons why it appears to justify further careful examination. In customary parlance, the credit instrument under study here is known as the commercial and industrial loan--a category often abbreviated as "C + I loans," or simply as "business loans." Within that category, attention is focused primarily, though not exclusively, on *short-term* business credits; i.e., loans with maturities ranging up to one year. After first tracing the basic facts about the size of this loan market in the United States, we consider where it fits into the respective financial activities of lenders and borrowers, and also observe the general course of interest rates up to the present time.

It will be argued here that the short-term bank loan to commercial and industrial firms is an instrument that derives its significance and merits study for two main reasons: *first*, because of the large volume of these loans, in absolute terms and in relation to the financial operations of both the banking industry itself and the business firms that are the borrowers; and *second*, because of the discussions in recent years about how bank loans are priced and about the current levels of those prices (interest rates).

As the book progresses, therefore, it seeks to widen and deepen the scope to analyze the factors governing the determination of interest rates on bank loans to business firms, and to explore some connections between bank lending and the functioning of other financial and economic phenomena.

The lending that commercial banks extend to business firms is such a basic part of banking operations that it figures in the very concept and definition of the term "bank." In the Definitions paragraphs of the Bank Holding Company Act of 1984, the Congress defined a bank as an institution "which (1) accepts deposits that the depositor has a legal right to withdraw on demand, and (2) engages in the business of making commercial loans." This legalistic definition was somewhat elaborated but essentially reaffirmed three years later in further legislation, which has been upheld juridically and in which the Federal Reserve concurs.[1] In addition to this statutory denotation, the important role played by the commercial and industrial loan is also reflected in the more nuanced usage and terminology of professional economics.[2]

Size of the Short-term Business Loan Market

For measuring the magnitude of the market for bank loans to commercial and industrial firms in the U.S., several pertinent sets of data are available. Some of these are more useful for analytical purposes than others; and in some cases there is a lack of correspondence between the coverage or definition employed in one set of data and those in another that should ideally be identical. For example, quarterly surveys conducted by the Federal Reserve provide figures on the volume of new business loans issued by domestically chartered commercial banks, broken down between short-term and long-term loans, and showing various details on the interest rates involved. Fed data applicable to the same group of banks are also published that give the volume of C + I loans *outstanding* on a monthly and even weekly basis, but provide no division according to maturities and no interest-rate figures. Nevertheless, the amount of information available is sufficient to permit a satisfactory assessment of the main characteristics of the short-term loan market.

Utilizing a data series inaugurated in its present form in 1977--the Survey of Terms of Bank Lending--one can establish a first approximation of the comparative volume of the two main maturity-groups of business loans: those with maturities under one year, and those one year and over. For 1977, the Federal Reserve quarterly survey data showed that a weekly average of $6.2 billion of short-term business loans was issued, and \$1.2 billion of long-term loans. A somewhat similar ratio was reported in the 1980s, with 1989 showing \$43.7 billion new short- and \$4.2 billion new long-term loans

TABLE 2.1 Comparative Volume of New Short- and Long-Term C+I Loans Made by Commercial Banks, 1977-1989 (billions of dollars)

Dollar Volume of Loans Made	*Average of Quarterly Survey Weeks in:*[a]				
	1977	*1981*	*1985*	*1987*	*1989*
Short-term	6.163	20.973	34.756	41.347	43.726
Long-term	1.161	3.017	5.183	5.055	4.191
TOTAL commercial and industrial	7.324	23.990	39.939	46.402	47.910
Short-term share (%)	84	87	87	89	91

a. This survey on terms of lending to business firms collects data on gross loans made during the first full business week in the mid-month of each quarter by a sample of commercial banks of all sizes. From the sample, the Board estimates the volume and other terms at all insured commercial banks. (Volume figures are averages calculated from data as published. Some later tables make adjustment reducing influence of overnight loans.)

Source: Data published quarterly in this breakdown by Board of Governors only since 1977.

made per week. Indeed, over the period 1977-1989 the percentage of short-term C + I loans rose gradually from 84 percent of the total to 91 percent (Table 2.1).

The Board of Governors had collected, since 1919, certain data on the interest rates charged by *large* U.S. banks on new loans to business firms. Until 1977, however, the information published from these quarterly surveys did not include anything on volume or maturities, and was indeed limited to weighted-average rates on all loans made during the survey period for maturities up to one year by large commercial banks (though coverage of large banks was progressively increased and improved by refined sampling). Thus we cannot trace quantitatively, from available data, whatever fluctuation may have occurred in earlier periods in the ratio between short and long maturities. For the most recent five years, we shall be able at a later stage to present some evidence on variations in maturity distribution, with the aid of breakdowns introduced in 1985.

Some further explanation seems pertinent regarding the body of data just referred to, which constitutes a major statistical source employed in this study.[3] The short-term loan section of the survey is composed of two main parts, one distributed by maturity groups: overnight; one month and under; over one month and under a year; and demand loans. The other main part shows the same loan volume but divided between fixed-rate and floating-rate loans, with each of those rate types broken down by size of loan. For both of the above main parts and their subgroups, the column headings show the volume of loans made; average size; weighted average maturity; weighted average effective interest rate; and two rough dispersion measures. (Certain auxiliary information included will be considered at a later stage.)

For purposes of analysis, the cardinal advantage of the information generated by the Survey of Terms of Bank Lending (STBL) is that it provides both quantity and price data for new loan transactions between bank lenders and nonbank borrowers that take place at a limited, 5-day point in time. This information, which is not found in other periodic series on bank loan operations, is of particular value in examining the known, or possible, relationships between business borrowing (= bank lending) and the contemporaneous movements in other sectors of the financial markets (and, *a fortiori*, movements in macroeconomic variables) whose data are quoted regularly in time series. How do interest rates on business loans behave in contrast to commercial paper rates? Do loan rates change as the volume of loans changes? What light do these data shed on the presumed relation between interest-rate and price-level movements, or on the behavior of lending (= borrowing) rates at banks during various paces of general economic growth or points in the business cycle? Other desirable features of the STLB are that the data collected on loan terms are now presented not only for short-term business loans in the aggregate but also for four different maturity groups and for fixed- and floating-rate loans totaled separately; and that, despite the effort required in collecting and manipulating this amount of illuminating detail, the quarterly data appear frequently enough to provide, in most periods, a satisfactory tracking of price and quantity movements in the commercial loan market.

Certain limitations also deserve to be noted. One that the Fed is careful to volunteer is that the STLB figures *sui generis* measure lending terms that prevail in a single designated, predetermined week in each quarter. As the central bank points out, the resulting numbers do not necessarily represent terms applicable to the entire quarter concerned. In addition, the reliance on a 5-day, chosen week opens the possibility that random factors within or external to the loan market in the designated week could produce an atypically high or low result in loan pricing or (more likely) volume. While the author has observed some minor instances of this effect, the averaging of the four quarterly data produces annual figures that appear to exhibit fairly high credibility; and this risk probably can be more closely detected in later tables and charts using the quarterly numbers themselves.

Another limitation that deserves special mention has to do with the phenomenon of overnight loans. The revisions carried out by the Federal Reserve in 1977, as mentioned above, introduced reporting on long-term business loans and altered the sample of reporting banks to include institutions of all sizes. The breakdown of the short-term loans by maturities, however, was not begun until February 1985. Prior to that time, the figures calculated on average maturity of short-term loans issued in the survey week and on the weighted average interest rate referred to *all* loans in the short category--from one day (overnight) to 364 days. The Fed was aware of the fact that an overnight loan typically carries an interest rate that is low and is often priced from a different reference, or basing, rate than longer-term credits. In addition, for some borrowers, a portion of the loans designated as overnights is renewed one or more times, yielding the possibility that in a given STLB survey week an undetermined number of overnight loans might be rolled over (and counted) as many as five times. To the extent, that occurred, the total volume of reported new loans would be raised, and the weighted average interest rate would be lowered.

The separation into four maturity groups, starting in 1985, permitted the computation of an average rate for each of the maturity groups, of course; and for certain purposes it will be pertinent below to refer to one or another of those groups. For other purposes the focus is on the lending terms applicable to short-term business loans in the aggregate. Federal Reserve staff experts recognize that some downward adjustment of the reported volume of overnights should be applied in calculating the weighted interest rate for total short-term loans, but have felt unable to decide, for their own use or for advising others, just where the indicated adjustment divisor should lie on a scale from 1.1 to 5.0. The author, summoning sufficient courage or rashness, has adopted an adjustment divisor of 2.0 for reducing the reported volume of overnight loans in such cases. In those instances, the fact will be noted in the table or text. Obviously, the volume adjustment can be calculated only for the disaggregated STLB data published since 1985.[4]

In identifying published data sources that provide some information with reference to the commercial and industrial loans of the banking system, one must mention the vast amount of balance-sheet material collected by the Federal Reserve, much of which is published in different degrees of detail and frequency. The dollar figures appear in fullest detail in the Consolidated Report of Condition (sometimes referred to as the "call report") that is published four times per year and contains figures on assets and liabilities for all insured commercial banks and for different breakdowns thereof by size, Federal Reserve membership, and other methods of classification. Utilizing this material, an annual article is published in the *Federal Reserve Bulletin* that analyzes for the previous year the consolidated balance sheet and income statement of the banking system. In addition to absolute dollar amounts of the various asset categories, a considerable number of ratios are computed to show, *e.g.*, interest income for the year as a percentage of average consolidated assets. The orientation of that annual report is reflected in the title, "The Profitability of Insured Commercial Banks in 1987," and it is valuable for measuring industry profits.[5] For purposes of the present study, these consolidated reports of condition provide useful portfolio information on the volume of C + I loans (and other loan categories) outstanding at the dates given. The only information related to loan income, however, is in the form of annual dollar or percentage figures derived for the year as a whole from the above-mentioned financial statements, and these cannot identify the specific dates or terms of the many loan transactions reflected in the portfolio.

From Table 2.1 we have observed the predominant share of short-term loans in total bank lending to commercial and industrial firms. Two other measures of the relative magnitude of short-term business loans provide additional indications of their importance. For gauging the size of C + I loans in comparison with other types of lending by banks, one must turn to the consolidated balance-sheet sources referred to in the preceding paragraph, since the quarterly survey of terms on new loans is not conducted for all types of bank loans. During the five years 1985 through 1989, the volume of C + I loans (of all maturities) outstanding at U.S. commercial banks amounted to 30 to 32 percent of all loans in their portfolios, equaling the 32 percent recorded in both 1977 and 1979. Until 1986, the C + I category was the largest of the four types among which total bank loans (excluding interbank credits) are statistically distributed. Real estate loans began in 1986 to exceed business loans, though their gains in the period 1986-1989 have been accompanied by reductions in the shares of loans to "individuals" and "all other," rather than in the C + I share. The real estate category on the consolidated condition report includes mortgage lending to both commercial and residential borrowers, as well as loans to developers; and the recent growth of commercial bank lending in the real estate category reflects in part the decline in the savings and loan industry in the 1980s (see Table 2.2). Thus, loans of less than a one-year maturity continue to be the major type of borrowing at banks by commercial and industrial firms; and the short business loan is the major type of *short-term* lending by banks to any client group.

In appraising the importance of short-term borrowing from banks as a source of financing for the commercial and industrial sector, it is relevant to compare the borrowing from banks with the volume of funding obtained from the securities markets. In order to make this comparison, it is assumed that the arithmetic mean of the amounts of new short-term business loans made in the four quarterly survey weeks can be taken as roughly approximating the average weekly volume for the year concerned. These averages were tabulated for the years 1985-1989, together with statistics compiled by the Federal Reserve from governmental and private sources on the volume of corporate bonds and stocks issued in those years, the yearly totals being first converted to weekly averages. In computing the volume of corporate securities issued, all industry groups were included with the exception of the group "real estate and financial" for both bonds and stocks. That group was excluded in order to achieve approximate comparability between the coverage of

TABLE 2.2 Loans Outstanding at Domestically Chartered Commercial Banks, by Category, 1985-89 (end of year, billions of dollars)

	1985	1986	1987	1988	1989
Total loans, excluding interbank	1,399.2	1,536.1	1,606.7	1,732.3	2,015.3
Commercial and industrial	446.6	487.7	479.1	500.6	639.4
Real estate	421.7	495.9	580.8	654.3	757.7
Of which, revolving credit	N.A.	N.A.	31.7	40.1	49.1
Individual	299.5	321.5	334.8	361.1	384.5
All other	231.5	230.9	212.0	216.3	233.8
Percent distribution:					
Total loans, excluding interbank	100.0	100.0	100.0	100.0	100.0
Commercial and industrial	31.9	31.8	29.8	28.9	31.7
Real estate	30.1	32.3	36.2	37.8	37.6
Of which, revolving credit	N.A.	N.A.	2.0	2.3	2.4
Individual	21.4	20.9	20.8	20.9	19.1
All other	16.6	15.0	13.2	12.5	11.6

N.A. Not available.

Source: Federal Reserve Bulletin.

long-term security issuance by business borrowers and the coverage of short-term bank borrowing by commercial and industrial firms, which excludes interbank loans and real estate loans.

Not surprisingly, the volume of outside financing by corporations varies in volume from year to year, in response to fluctuations in the level of economic activity, the amount of self-financing available from gross income, the comparative present and anticipated interest rates in the respective markets, etc. In all five years, however, the average weekly volume of short-term bank loans considerably exceeded the amount of stocks and bonds issued. When the bank lending figures are adjusted by excluding one-half the reported amount of overnight loans, the adjusted volume of bank lending ranged from about 7.5 to over 20 times the combined stock and bond flotations (Table 2.3).

This obviously is not meant to imply that the short-term loan market is 7 to 20 times "more important" than the securities markets. The two markets serve different but important needs in financing the flow of funds to and from the corporate world. Money raised by business firms in the securities markets represents investment funds used, for example, to buy buildings and machinery or to acquire other firms, and becomes part of the permanent capital structure of the corporations concerned. The funds borrowed from commercial banks are employed for a wide variety of purposes--to finance inventories of materials or goods in process, payrolls and other employee-related costs, seasonal variations in cash flows, or the countless other "lead-and-lag" factors that affect the relationship between the current assets and current liabilities of the borrowing enterprises. In addition, corporations sometimes negotiate a bank loan to help, along withretained earnings, in temporarily financing an expansion until a bond or stock issue can be floated at more favorable terms.

The borrowing firms that require short-term financing for the purposes just described cover the entire range of the industrial structure. Behind the shorthand name "business loan" or "commercial loan" stands an extremely broad array of enterprises in the fields of manufacturing, transportation and communication, the extractive industries, services, and construction that fill their needs for working capital by borrowing, through C + I loans of varying maturities and at fixed or variable rates, at commercial banks. In the latest years for which statistics distributed

TABLE 2.3   Volume of New Short-Term C+I Loans Compared With New Securities Issued (weekly averages, in billions of dollars)

Type of Financing	1985	1986	1987	1988	1989
New Bonds Issued					
a. Total bonds	111.5	190.5	153.3	167.2	79.1
b. Weekly ave.					
(L.a/52)	2.1	3.7	2.9	3.2	1.5
New Stocks Issued					
c. Total stocks	19.3	33.9	35.0	20.0	12.8
d. Weekly ave.					
(L.c/52)	.372	.652	.673	.385	.246
e. Stocks and bonds,					
combined	2.5	4.3	3.6	3.6	1.8
New Short-Term C + I					
Loans by Banks					
f. Ave. of 4 surveys,					
as reported	34.8	40.8	41.3	44.7	43.7
g. Ratio to Line e	13.8	9.5	11.4	12.4	24.7
h. Ave. of 4 surveys,					
with adjustment					
reducing overnights	27.4	32.4	34.2	38.1	38.2
i. Ratio to Line e	10.9	7.5	9.4	10.6	21.6

Figures in Lines a and c are for all corporate groups, except real estate and financial group.

Source: Calculated from data on issues of U.S. corporations collected by IDD Information Services, Inc., Board of Governors, and U.S. Securities and Exchange Commission, as published in *Federal Reserve Bulletin.* Data on C + I loans from source listed in Table 2.1.

across industries were published, the largest group of borrowers was in the field of trade and distribution, with 18 percent of total loans outstanding at the large weekly reporting banks that account for nearly two-thirds of all domestic business loans. Other major borrowing groups were durable goods manufacturing, nondurable goods manufacture, and the broad services sector (Table 2.4). Note that the source supplying this distribution by industry also provides our only source of data breaking down the loans outstanding (at large banks) by original maturity. As expected, the division between short- and long-term loans is roughly even, whereas for new-loan origination Table 2.1 showed that loans written for less than one year account for nearly 90 percent. These relationships require the banks and the supervisory authorities to exercise some caution with regard to interest-rate risk, though much less so than in the case of real estate loans.

For these nonfinancial business firms, the interest paid to banks for providing this working capital constitutes an operating cost that, along with other elements, enters into the considerations determining the pricing of their products or services. For the commercial banks as lenders of working-capital funds, moreover, the interest rate charged on short-term loans to business firms constitutes a price, the level of which is influenced by various considerations that include the lending rates prevailing at competitive financial institutions and the cost of funds that the banks themselves are paying, as intermediaries, to their depositors and certificate holders.

Interest on Business Loans Since 1950: A First Overview

After having reviewed several measures of the magnitude and role of the short-term loans made by U.S. commercial banks to business firms, this chapter will close with a first examination of the interest rates prevailing in this market, and their movements over the past 40 years. This broad overview, commencing with data expressed on an annual basis, will provide a background for later explorations utilizing more detailed breakdowns and more frequent observations. Those will endeavor to contribute, empirically as well as theoretically, to a better understanding of the forces influencing business-loan rates, or exerted in turn by them.

The building of a continuous statistical series of average rates on short-term business loans can be accomplished by employing the figures published by the Survey of Terms of Bank Lending described above for the years 1977 to date, together with those of the predecessors of that series for earlier years. Since statistical time series--like most man-made structures--undergo renovation or remodeling in the course of their lifetime, a brief explanation is desirable on the extent of comparability of these data over

TABLE 2.4 C+I Loans Outstanding at Large Commercial Banks, by Industry Groups, 1977-1979[a] (billions of dollars)

Industry Group of Borrower	Last Wednesday in December			Ave. of 3 Decembers	
	1977	1978	1979	Dollars	Percent
Durable goods manufacturing	15.8	18.2	23.6	19.2	16.3
Nondurable goods manuftg.	15.7	17.7	19.2	17.5	14.9
Mining (including crude oil and natural gas)	8.6	10.1	12.0	10.2	8.7
Trade and distribution	18.0	21.5	24.9	21.5	18.3
Transportation, communication and other utilities	12.6	13.8	17.8	14.7	12.5
Construction	4.7	5.3	5.8	5.3	4.5
Services	12.2	15.6	19.4	15.7	13.3
All other[b]	12.0	14.3	14.8	13.7	11.6
Total domestic C + I loans	99.8	116.4	137.5	117.8	100.0
Memo: Loans with original maturity one year or more included in total[c]	49.0	56.8	72.4		

[a] Data refer to C + I loans made by large weekly reporting banks with domestic assets of $1 billion or more at December 1977, and exclude foreign loans.

[b] Includes miscellaneous borrowers, as well as loans at a few banks that do not classify their loans.

[c] This line included here because this source provides the only published series (for 1972-1979 only) showing a breakdown of outstanding loans between long- and short-term.

Source: Board of Governors, Annual Statistical Digest, 1970-1979.

time. For purposes of the present study, the period between the start of collection by the Federal Reserve of interest-rates on loans (1919) and 1948 can be omitted, owing particularly to the special conditions that prevailed in financial markets during, first, the Great Depression of the 1930s and then during World War II. From 1948 through 1976, the nature and characteristics of the Fed's business loan survey remained substantially the same, especially as affects the average rates. The instrument to be reported was the commercial and industrial loan of less than one-year maturity; respondents reported rate data for each new loan made during the survey period, which was originally the first two weeks in the last month of each quarter; weighted averages were computed from the raw figures, with a breakdown provided by size of loan; and the reporting sample comprised a selected group of *large* banksthroughout the country. Part-way through that period, in 1967, revisions were carried out that increased the size of the reporting sample of banks, created a breakdown by six geographic areas, and shifted the collection dates of the four surveys from the last month in the quarter to the middle month. None of the foregoing changes has appeared to alter the behavior or damage the comparability over time of the average interest rates produced, in the opinion of the author and the Federal Reserve staff.[6]

More recently, modifications were introduced at successive revision dates. Commencing at the beginning of 1977, the sample was divided, so as to show weighted interest rates for large banks, as always before, but now also for all banks. At the same time, additional information began to be collected and published, including estimated loan volume at all commercial banks, blown up from data gathered in the survey period (now shortened from two weeks to one), and average maturity and other details on terms. Finally, starting in 1985, the published survey has been presenting the results with two breakdowns, one by size of loan and an added one by maturity groups. In Figure 2.1, one curve shows the weighted average interest rate on new C + I loans at all commercial banks for the period 1977 through 1991; and the other curve shows the corresponding average for large banks from 1950 through 1991, both lines being annual weighted averages.

The high similarity between the movements of the two curves, during the period in which both sets of averages are available, is evident in tabular as well as graphic presentations. Of the thirteen years 1977-1989, the weighted average rate on business loans made at large

20

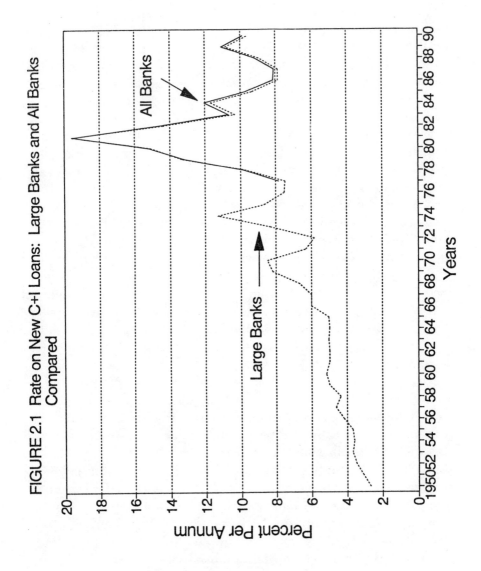

FIGURE 2.1 Rate on New C+I Loans: Large Banks and All Banks Compared

TABLE 2.5 Comparative Rates on Short-Term C+I Loans at Large Banks and All Banks, 1977-1989
(weighted average in percent per annum)

Date		Average Rate in Survey Week of:				Annual Average	Large Banks Relative to All Banks: Arithmetic Deviation	Ratio (in percent)
		February	May	August	November			
1977	All	7.50	7.40	7.80	8.62	7.83		
	Large	7.00	7.01	7.49	8.43	7.48	-0.35	95.53
1978	All	8.90	8.96	9.92	11.44	9.81		
	Large	8.67	8.79	9.76	11.46	9.67	-0.14	98.57
1979	All	12.27	12.34	12.31	15.81	13.18		
	Large	12.35	12.32	12.48	16.23	13.33	0.15	101.14
1980	All	15.67	17.75	11.56	15.71	15.17		
	Large	15.77	17.44	11.18	15.76	15.04	-0.13	99.14
1981	All	19.91	19.99	21.11	17.23	19.56		
	Large	20.06	20.16	21.16	16.88	19.57	0.01	100.05
1982	All	17.13	17.11	13.27	11.26	14.69		
	Large	17.05	16.97	12.68	10.81	14.38	-0.31	97.89
1983	All	10.20	10.31	11.09	10.95	10.64		
	Large	9.85	9.93	10.85	10.62	10.31	-0.33	96.90
1984	All	11.06	12.45	13.29	11.29	12.02		
	Large	10.78	12.16	13.07	10.84	11.71	-0.31	97.42

(continued)

Year	Type						Deviation	Ratio
1985	All	10.10	9.86	9.28	9.68	9.73	-0.38	96.09
	Large	9.71	9.37	8.91	9.39	9.35		
1986	All	9.33	8.13	7.73	7.28	8.12	-0.27	96.67
	Large	9.03	7.83	7.46	7.07	7.85		
1987	All	7.46	8.24	8.20	8.47	8.09	-0.22	97.28
	Large	7.25	8.03	7.98	8.20	7.87		
1988	All	8.37	8.49	9.75	10.11	9.18	-0.19	97.93
	Large	8.07	8.32	9.55	10.00	8.99		
1989	All	10.97	11.89	10.78	10.50	11.04	-0.20	98.19
	Large	10.86	11.63	10.64	10.23	10.84		
	Average deviation or ratio:						-0.21%	97.91

Source: Calculated from data in *Federal Reserve Bulletin* and statistical releases.

banks lay slightly below that at all banks in eleven years. The mean of these negative deviations was about one-fourth of one percentage point (-0.26 percent). For all 13 years, the mean of all deviations, positive and negative, was -0.21 percent; and the mean of the ratios of large-bank interest rates to all-bank rates was 97.91 percent (Table 2.5). In view of this degree of parallelism, it seems justifiable, in instances for which it is desired to make use of a historical interest-rate series, to regard the series on average loan ratesat large banks as an acceptable surrogate for an all-bank series over the period prior to 1977, especially for exercises employing data in annual form.[7]

If we proceed on that basis, certain broad observations about the course of lending rates on business loans can be stated at this stage. The post-war years of the 1950s constituted a period in which loan rates exhibited remarkable stability within a narrow, low range. World War II had occasioned a variety of exceptional governmental measures involving allocation of raw materials, rationing, price controls, etc. that had constraining effects on the pricing process in financial as well as nonfinancial markets. In the five years from 1943 through 1947, the banks made loans to business firms at rates that averaged between 2.1 percent in the lowest to 2.6 percent in the highest year. As the adjustment later from a wartime economy proceeded, this interest rate average moved very slowly higher, not reaching an annual mean of four percent until 1956. During the eleven years from 1957 through 1967, a new semi-plateau of narrow movements established itself, with the annual average moving only between the 4.5 and 6.0 percent levels.

Within the span of years after the 1960s, however, the lending rates on business loans entered a different period, of as-yet-unknown duration, in which the fluctuations have been larger and more frequent, and have reached higher peaks than at any time since the Federal Reserve began collecting such data in 1919. An excursion into higher ground began in 1968, and the lending rate in 1969 and 1970 reached nearly 8.5 percent before it declined to the plus-or-minus 6 percent range for 1971-1972. From that point on, the business loan rate in the 1970s and 1980s registered frequent swings; in a few cases the annual average rose or fell three to five full percentage points from one year to the next. In rare instances the changes from one quarter to the next one measured four to six percentage points.

A first examination of the data on bank lending rates readily indicates that in the last 18-20 years, the interest rates on business loans have exhibited levels and fluctuations which, by historical comparisons, could be regarded as "high" and "abnormal." In looking at the course traced during the post-War period as a whole, one can distinguish roughly certain sub-periods and perhaps even identify approximately the more critical areas in the pattern. But examining the interest-rate data alone does not provide us with explanations. On the contrary, it raises many questions and induces one to look much further. Is the recent behavior of loan rates the result of microeconomic factors operating in the banking industry itself, such as some new instability in the demand for short-term credit? How do business loan rates compare with the movement of other interest rates? If they have been moving similarly, is there some basic non-bank factor that is driving all interest rates in the economy? For example, could such an underlying force be the rate of economic growth; or the fiscal stance of the Federal government and its consequences on the volume of government borrowing? What is the relationship between the interest that banks pay to depositors and the rate they charge to borrowers, and how has this cost of funds behaved? What, if any, are the implications of commercial bank lending rates for the conduct of monetary policy by the central bank? And, on the more abstract level of monetary theory, what is the process by which interest rates (or *the* interest rate?) are determined?

The following chapter will begin addressing some of these questions.

Notes

1. See 12 USCS 1841, Definitions (c); and 12 CFR 225.145. The Federal Reserve's need to participate in defining commercial loans and the banks that extend them arises from the necessity to establish which financial institutions in the U.S. are subject to the Fed's jurisdiction and supervision, in general; and in particular to determine which types of transaction or activity can be performed only by banks thus defined (i.e., the "bank *v.* nonbank" problem).

2. "Commercial banks are the dominant institution in the financial sector of the economy and one of the most important institutions in the overall economy." Kaufman, 1973: p. 61. "In a world of ever-changing financial institutions, the making of commercial loans is used to define and identify that which constitutes a commercial bank." Estrella, 1986: p. 159. For a more qualified, "non-definitive" characterization, see David W. Pearce (ed.), *The MIT Dictionary of Modern Economics*, Cambridge, The MIT Press, 1986, p. 69.

3. As described by the Survey itself in 1990, it currently "...collects data on gross loan extensions made during the first full business week in the mid-month of each quarter by a sample of 340 commercial banks of all sizes.... The sample

data are blown up to estimate the lending terms at all insured commercial banks during that week. The estimated terms of bank lending are not intended" to represent "the terms of loans extended over the entire quarter or residing in the portfolios of those banks. Mortgage loans, purchased loans, foreign loans, and loans of less than $1,000 are excluded from the Survey." Federal Reserve Statistical Release E.2, Survey of Terms of Bank Lending Made During February 5-9, 1990, dated March 22, 1990.

4. In Table 2.1, the dollar volume of short-term business loans was presented as reported in the STLB, in order to preserve comparability between the pre-1985 years and the years for which we have the data to adjust the overnights. If the adjusted figures for 1985, 1987, and 1989 had been employed, the percentage share of short-term in total business loans for those years would be 84 percent, 87 percent, and 90 percent instead of 87 percent, 89 percent, and 91 percent, respectively.

5. See *e.g.*, Mary M. McLaughlin and Martin H. Wolfson, 1988, pp. 403-418. More abbreviated but still comprehensive reports on the composite assets and liabilities of both domestically-chartered and all banking institutions in the U.S. are issued monthly in the *Bulletin*.

6. See e.g., Board of Governors, *Banking and Monetary Statistics, 1941-1970*, "Series Beginning 1966," pp. 642-645.

7. This assumption reflects the judgment that, since the two series exhibit a fairly close and stable relationship over the last 13 years and since the construction and manipulation of the data have not been changed in a manner materially affecting the ability of the respective averages to represent the statistical universes concerned, one may assume that the ability of the large-bank series to represent average rates at all banks applies also to pre-1977 years.

3

More Dimensions:
Loans Held vs. Loans Originated

The preceding chapter traced the uneven swings by which the interest rate on bank loans to commercial and industrial firms moved, in the 1970s and 1980s, into distinctly higher levels and generally sustained that elevation, despite some marked fluctuations. Some corporate firms that are the customers in this loan market have been discontented with their borrowing costs and, besides voicing occasional complaints, have explored alternative sources of credit, both from domestic financial institutions and from foreign banking centers. Indeed, some analysts find presumptive evidence that American commercial banks may not be maintaining their relative share of the business loan market--whether because of the lending rate or because of other ingredients in the competitive mixture. The alternative financial sources that are, to varying degrees, available to borrowing firms are principally the investors in commercial paper, foreign banks, and, to a limited extent since 1982, savings and loan associations.

Concern about the behavior of interest rates is not confined, of course, to the corporations that are the borrowers of commercial loans. The Federal government, for its part, has continuing and legitimate reasons for watching and projecting the course of interest rates, starting with the government's own budget costs for any net borrowing it anticipates. Beyond the direct fiscal requirements of the government, however, the Congress and the executive branch follow interest-rate movements for their possible effects on the growth and stability of the private economy. In that context, the government's focus is not uniquely on the C + I loan rate (or any other single rate) but on "interest rates" collectively. Historically, the viewpoint of political leaders in the United States has reflected a predisposition against interest levels that could be regarded as high or excessive, terms that are not often clearly defined. This attitude, while not to be equated with that of the extreme populists, led to the enactment in various states of laws on usury. It also contributed to provisions, in the Banking Act of 1933, authorizing the Federal Reserve Board to set ceilings to the interest rates that banks could pay on time and savings deposits. Those ceilings, applied through the Board's Regulation Q, remained in force from 1933 until they were progressively phased out, under federal legislation, in the early 1980s.[1]

From time to time throughout the post-World War II period, the sensitivity to interest-rate considerations in Washington has reached the point of anxiety, and at such moments it frequently takes the form of implied or outright criticism of the Federal Reserve's monetary policy stance and a call for an easing of that position. Of equal frequency is a quite different contention, namely, that the present level of the whole interest-rate structure is mainly the result of the large, persistent deficits in the Federal budget and that it cannot be altered significantly until that deficit is drastically reduced.

Before passing in later sections of the book to consider the broader connections just mentioned, we examine in the present chapter the developments in regard to business loans in the commercial banking industry itself and in its closer competitors.

Short-term Business Credit: Volume Outstanding

Analysis of the position of the commercial banks as suppliers of short-term loans to business firms can be approached from different directions. The basis most frequently used is by reference to statistical series on the dollar volume of loans outstanding at the pertinent dates. For all insured commercial banks, the Federal Reserve has a continuous series on the total volume of loans outstanding to commercial and industrial firms that is substantially comparable in composition from 1959 to the present (and somewhat less comparable for the interval 1948-1959.[2] The series covers both short- and long-term commercial loans together, and, unfortunately for our purposes, separate data on short-term commercial credits are not available. Nevertheless, as shown previously in Chapter 2, a very high proportion of business loans issued is in the short, less-than-a-year category.

The volume of business loans grew steadily but fairly slowly in current dollar terms in the late 1960s and early 1970s, rising from an average volume of $90 billion in 1968 to $169 billion in 1976; the latter figure represented a slight decline during the recession of 1975-1976. From 1977 onward, the business loan portfolio of the commercial banks rose continuously through the end of the 1980s, save for a drop of about $30 billion in the brief recession in 1980. During this period 1977-1989, outstanding business loans climbed from $199 billion to $510 billion (annual averages), an increase of 156 percent in current dollars, or 36.4 percent in constant dollars (Figure 3.1).

For comparison, Figure 3.1 also charts the growth, for the period since 1967, of loans outstanding to nonfinancial firms in the commercial paper market. Since credit obtained through the issuance of commercial paper is regarded as currently constituting the principal competitor to the C + I loan issued by the banking industry, it is necessary to identify the definitional questions involved in choosing a series on commercial paper. Owing to the methods of operation peculiar to the issuance of commercial paper, as contrasted to bank lending, the methods of classifying and reporting on the volume outstanding in that market also differ from the banking statistics. Some of these classification questions are pertinent to the present study, while others are immaterial in this context. They all stem from the nature of the note instrument itself and the manner in which the borrowing transaction between lender and borrower is effectuated in a given case.

The term "commercial paper" is a collective expression that refers to promissory notes (predominantly very short-term) drawn by the borrower in favor of a named lender (or, rarely, in bearer form), and normally unsecured in the sense of marketable collateral. Instead of the note's being secured, the issuer must have an acceptably high credit rating from a recognized rating company, and thus the issuers tend to be large, well-connected firms. Some borrowers in this channel are nonfinancial corporations in fields such as manufacturing, transport, construction, etc; and 70-80 percent of the paper outstanding is issued by financial companies engaged primarily in re-lending, in fields such as mortgage lending, automotive sales or leasing, consumer loans, or underwriting. Data collected on the volume of commercial paper outstanding are published both with a breakdown between financial and nonfinancial issuers and with a partial separation between the notes that are "dealer-placed" (through brokers) with the investing purchaser and those directly placed without the intervention of brokers.[3]

As described in the published data series on commercial paper outstanding,[4] nonfinancial issuers of paper are firms operating in the same industrial sectors as the firms borrowing at short-term from

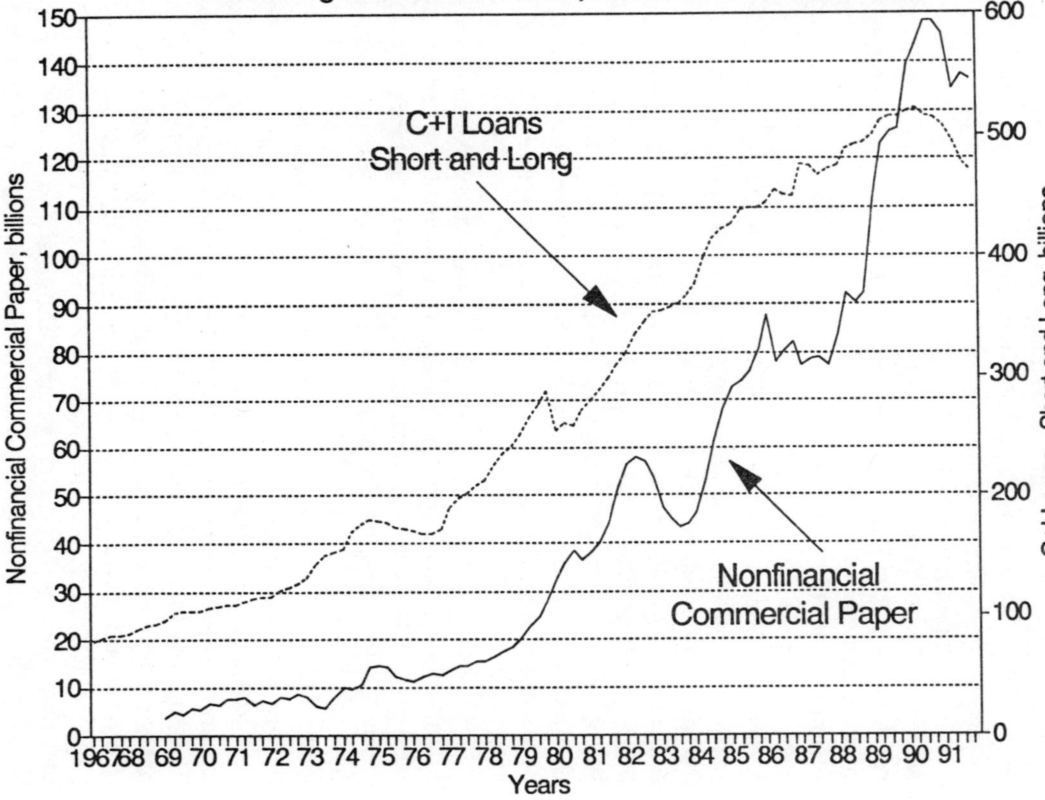

FIGURE 3.1 C+I Borrowing at Comercial Banks and Nonfinancial Company Borrowing in Commercial Paper; Volume Outstanding

banks, as tabulated in Table 2.4. While finance companies, which account for three-fourths of all notes issued in the paper market, compete with commercial banks for some types of lending or borrowing, their operations have little resemblance to those of enterprises that obtain short-term C + I loans from banks. In the author's judgment, the part of the paper market that is relevant to the subject of short-term borrowing by commercial and industrial firms is the paper issued by *nonfinancial* company borrowers, a view shared by most other research in that field.[5]

The volume of short-term loans to commercial and industrial firms that is generated in the commercial paper market is subject to greater fluctuation than occurs in loans made at commercial banks. While this is evident for the period covered by Figure 3.1, it has been characteristic for earlier decades as well. No single factor is sufficient to explain the more uneven growth of commercial paper financing, and it results from a variety of changing forces affecting one set of participants or another--the banks, the investors in commercial notes, and the potential borrowers–at one time or another. For example, during the mid- and late-1970s the commercial banks were experiencing chronic difficulties in maintaining a volume of deposits adequate to meet the rising loan demand, owing to the deposit interest-rate ceilings, which were raised several times but only after delays. This gave an impulse to business firms to borrow in short-term paper, producing a surge in paper outstanding that extended from 1977 through 1981. By 1982, the dismantling of the banks' rate ceilings on deposits was in full swing, and in addition the easing of the bond market permitted firms that had borrowed more at short-term than usual from the paper market to refinance on longer terms, and a marked downswing occurred in outstanding commercial paper.

Consolidating the available information on the amount of commercial credit outstanding from all lending sources is helpful in verifying the relative position of the banking industry. Table 3.1 presents for sample years from 1977 to 1989 the total end-of-year volume of outstanding business credit, as measured by the amounts owed to foreign banks, commercial paper holders, the savings and loan firms (since 1982), and domestically chartered commercial banks. The domestic banks are further broken down to show the volumes at the large (weekly reporting) banks, both in New York City and elsewhere; and all other domestic banks. (The sources do not separate short- from long-term loans.)

TABLE 3.1 Business Loans Outstanding at Commercial Banks and Other Credit Institutions in the U.S., 1977-1989 (end-December[a]; billions of dollars)

	1977		1985		1987		1989	
	$ Billion	Percent	$ Billion	Percent	$ Billion	Percent	$ Billion	Percent
All Commercial Banks	213.6	93.2	502.5	83.2	579.9	84.8	640.4	79.9
Domestic Banks	193.8	84.6	446.6	73.9	479.1	70.1	516.9	64.5
Weekly Reporting Banks	116.8	51.0	256.6	42.5	283.2	41.4	318.8	39.8
New York City	36.1	15.8	59.2	9.8	58.7	8.6	58.6	7.3
Outside New York City	80.7	35.2	197.3	32.7	224.5	32.8	260.2	32.5
Other Domestic Banks	77.0	33.6	190.0	31.5	195.9	28.7	198.1	24.7
Foreign Banks	19.8	8.6	55.9	9.3	100.8	14.7	123.5	15.4
FSLIC-insured Thrifts	0.0	0.0	16.4	2.7	22.6	3.3	31.6	3.9
Commercial Paper, nonfinancial issuers	15.5	6.8	85.0	14.1	81.2	11.9	129.8	16.2
Total Business Credit	229.1	100.0%	603.9	100.0%	683.7	100.0%	801.8	100.0%
Memo:								
Commercial paper, financial issuers	49.5		213.8		275.9		395.9	

a. Dollar figures on Lines 1 through 7 are for last Wednesday in month; those on Lines 8 and 9 are for last day of month.

Sources: Monthly and special tables in *Federal Reserve Bulletin*; statistical releases; Table V, Combined Financial Statements, Office of Thrift Supervision, 1989.

Each of these groups has registered a substantial increase in the dollar volume of business loans between 1977 and 1989. Relative shares in the market, however, have shifted in differing degrees over the 13-year period. Domestically chartered banks still account for the largest portion, by far, of the total, but have dropped from 84.6 to 64.5 percent. Within the domestic group, the large banks have declined less in percentage terms than the remainder of the domestics, some of which have merged with big banks. But within the group of large banks, the share of loans held at big New York City firms has decreased more markedly than that at large regional banks. The FSLIC-insured thrift institutions, which were empowered to extend commercial loans by federal legislation in 1982, entered the market thereafter, but their share of the total market in 1988 and 1989 reached only 4 percent, and seemed unlikely to grow. The two groups that gained in market share were the foreign-related banks and the commercial paper lenders, with 1977 percentage shares of 8.6 and 6.8 percent, respectively, rising to 15.4 and 16.2 percent in 1989.

To recapitulate, the data available on the volume of loans to the business sector show that, when measured by annual figures on the amounts outstanding at the three major groups of lending sources, all three continued throughout the 1970s and 1980s to make a large and growing amount of business loans. Investors in commercial paper and, to a slightly smaller extent, the foreign-related banks increased their relative shares in this type of lending over the period, with some year-to-year fluctuations. Commercial and industrial loans outstanding in the banking system continued to constitute the largest share, but clearly at a lower relative level than in the mid-1970s. These findings are consistent with those of other research employing balance-sheet data on outstanding loans.[6]

Short-term Business Credit: Volume Originated

Given the functional importance of the short-term loan as a source of finance to the private business sector, and given also the central place of that loan instrument, *ipso facto*, within the concept of commercial banking, it is desirable to ascertain whether other methods of measurement would substantiate the results based upon loans-outstanding data. This step is indicated as advisable for verifying the course of development of C + I loan volume and loan pricing within the banking industry itself and in relation to other sources of short-term financing. It will also be relevant to matters raised in later chapters concerning the relationships between price and quantity movements in the general economy and those in the banking field.

Fortunately, the desired alternative method of measurement is available by means of the data provided by the quarterly Survey of Terms of Bank Lending (STBL) conducted by the Federal Reserve, and described in Chapter 2. As explained there, the central bank started, in 1977, to collect information on the volume of new business loans, to supplement the data already being collected on the lending terms. We shall be using quarterly figures or annual averages from the STBL in various contexts throughout this study. For the immediate purpose, it is instructive to make a short tabulation showing the average dollar volume of gross new loans extended by domestically-chartered commercial banks in 1989 as compared with 1977, together with figures for the same two years on the volume of C & I loans outstanding. The annual average amount of outstanding business loans (short- and long-term) at the banks was $199 billion in 1977 and rose to $510 billion in 1989, a figure 2.56 times the earlier year. Over the same period, the average volume of new business loans made increased from somewhat over $7 billion per survey to about $48 billion, 6.54 times the base year. If stated in terms of constant (1982) dollars, the volume outstanding went up 36 percent while the amount of loan creation rose over 248 percent (Table 3.2). The same comparison can not be made with respect to either foreign banks or commercial paper, for data are not collected on the volume of newly made loans in those fields.

It is evident from the foregoing summary comparison that the volume of C + I loan creation over the last thirteen years grew at a much brisker pace than did the amount of loans outstanding. This raises some intriguing questions of interpretation. Is one series or the other simply deficient or "wrong"? Does the differential between their growth rates mean that the two different methods of measurement are inconsistent; or non-comparable; or complementary? Some of these questions can be answered partially or even satisfactorily.

Comparability of Coverage

Both the balance-sheet series on loans outstanding and the series on new loan extensions are collected by the Board of Governors from broad samples of domestically chartered commercial banks, and the data collected are blown up to represent the respective estimated aggregates for all domestically chartered and insured banks. Although the new-loan survey is based on a sample smaller than the other series, its data are collected from 340 banks of all sizes; and the standard error of the

TABLE 3.2 Change in Average Volume of C + I Loans Outstanding Compared With Change in Average Volume of New Loans Made, 1977 to 1989 (billions of dollars)

Year	Average Volume of Loans Outstanding[a]		Average Volume of New Loans Created[b]	
	Dollars	Volume Relative	Dollars	Volume Relative
1977	199.2	100.0	380.8	100.0
1989	510.0	256.0	2,491.3	654.2
In constant (1982) dollars:				
1977	296.0	100.0	565.9	100.0
1989	403.8	136.4	1,972.5	348.6

[a]Annual Average of monthly figures.
[b]Average of the four quarterly Survey of Terms of Lending survey weeks, annualized.

Sources: Federal Reserve Bulletin and statistical releases.

weighted-average interest rate calculated from those data, for the four most recent surveys, ranged narrowly from 0.14 to 0.16 percent. The fact that each of the STBL surveys gathers numbers for a single five-day week implies that the survey could occasionally fall on a week atypical of that quarter. This could be distorting if one were concentrating on the movement within a particular year but is unlikely to damage the long-term pattern that is under study here. Moreover, the series tallying the loans outstanding consists of a reading taken on an even narrower period--the last Wednesday of the month in question.

Variation in Maturity

A factor that could potentially explain the swifter growth of new-loan creation than of the banks' aggregate loan portfolio would be a change in the maturity of the loans being made. During periods of increased uncertainty or of elevated interest rates, corporations are known to borrow less at long-term through issuance of bonds and more in the form of short-term loans. Perhaps such considerations could have operated *within* the bank-loan market itself, so as to shorten the maturities of new loans and increase their frequency. From 1977 on, the STBL has gathered data on the average maturity of the loans made, with separate figures for short- and long-term loans. For the short-term credits, the weighted-average maturity was calculated from terms for all types of loans except those specifying no maturity (now known as demand loans). Included in the computation were the numbers on overnight loans as reported by the respondent banks, without an attempted adjustment for possible renewals within the survey week. Starting with 1985, the average terms began to be calculated for each of four different short-term types: overnight; one month and under; over one month and less than a year; and demand loans. While the demand loans and the overnights do not yield themselves to this process of calculating (at the time of data collection) an average maturity, the separate averages for the two other types assist in answering the question raised above (Table 3.3).

Within the space of the first five years for which dollar volume and maturity data are available, there was indeed a marked decline in the average length of the short-term C + I bank loan. Whereas the average loan in the period 1977-1979 was written with an original maturity of about 90 days, this fell rapidly to 73, 55, and 38 days in the years 1980, 1981, 1982, respectively. Thereafter, the average maturity has stayed in the 38-46 day range most of the time. It will be noted that the fairly stable maturity levels of the under-one-month and the month-to-one-year categories in the five years 1985 through 1989--at the same time that the overall maturity average was slightly rising--is explained by a small *relative* decline in the number of overnight loans reported during those years.

As pointed out in the preceding paragraph, the statistics presented in Table 3.3 show that, in the course of the period starting in 1977, changes did occur in the average maturity of the short-term business loans observed in the Board of Governors' STBL. After being stable in the first three years, the weighted-average length decreased rapidly in the next three years, following which it established a new plateau at a level of 43-50 days--somewhat higher than its low point of about 38 days in 1982-1984. Just how much did these changes, particularly the lower portion of the average maturity curve, affect the data on total yearly volume of new loans, and how much of the upward slope of loan volume is due to other factors?

TABLE 3.3 Average Maturities of Short-term C + I Loans

	Weighted Average Maturity (days)			Memo	Average Size per Loan	
Date	All Short-Term as Reported	1 Month and Under	Under 1 Year	Average Maturity, Long-term Loans (mos.)	In Current Dollars	In Constant 1982 Dollars
1977	93	N.A.	N.A.	45.3	46,867	69,639
1978	89	N.A.	N.A.	44.7	51,810	71,759
1979	89	N.A.	N.A.	47.4	54,594	69,458
1980	73	N.A.	N.A.	44.5	83,769	97,747
1981	55	N.A.	N.A.	47.7	129,065	137,449
1982	38	N.A.	N.A.	48.5	215,610	215,610
1983	37	N.A.	N.A.	53.8	213,037	205,040
1984	38	N.A.	N.A.	49.2	210,060	194,861
1985	44	17	144	51.8	205,920	185,514
1986	43	18	140	53.0	281,750	247,583
1987	46	17	141	51.5	300,250	255,750
1988	46	17	135	50.5	315,500	260,099
1989	51	17	133	49.0	295,000	233,571

Sources: Calculated from quarterly survey reports of STBL, Board of Governors.

For addressing this question, the estimated annual total volume of new short-term loans was obtained by annualizing the STBL data, and that total for each year was adjusted by relating it to the average loan maturity for that year. The resulting maturity-adjusted figure was then corrected for price-level changes (Table 3.4). Manipulated in these two operations, the series displays an upward movement more gradual than the original data as collected, but nevertheless it indicates that short-term business loans, on this basis of constant dollars and constant maturity length, reached a volume about 81 percent higher in 1989 than in 1977. This compares with the rise, over those same years, in the volume of C + I loans outstanding (adjusted for price changes only) of 36 percent. Although data are not available to permit adjusting the latter series for maturity changes, of course, it is certain that the banking system's C + I portfolio was also affected, to some indeterminate degree, by the reduced maturity of new loans being issued. With the effects of maturity variation and price changes eliminated, the 81 percent growth in the origination of short-term C + I loans can be attributed to their increased number and size.

Variation in Loan Size

While the average maturity of short-term business loans was executing the decline and subsequent partial recovery described in the preceding paragraphs, change was also occurring in the average dollar amount of the loans being originated. The right-hand panel of Table 3.3 shows that during the three years 1977-1979 the average size in real terms (1982 dollars) was about $70,000. From 1980 through the rest of the decade, the size per loan increased at an uneven pace, reaching $260,000 in constant dollars in 1988. For the period since 1985, one can verify this rising size per loan by reference to the breakdown by type in the Board of Governors' survey (omitting the overnight loans, for reasons given).

Having reviewed in greater detail the data available on the volume of new short-term bank loans to commercial and industrial firms, one can conclude that they confirm a genuine growth in real terms of this type of lending by the commercial banking system, and at a pace that exceeds the growth indicated by the standard data on loans outstanding.

TABLE 3.4 New Short-term Loans Made by Commercial Banks, Adjusted for Changes in Maturities and Price Level (billions of dollars)

	1977	1978	1979	1987	1988	1989
New short-term loans made: weekly average, as reported	6.163	7.642	7.957	34.2	38.1	38.2
1. Estimated annual total	320.5	397.4	413.8	1,778.4[a]	1,981.2[a]	1,986.4[a]
2. Weighted ave. maturity (days)[b]	93	89	89	46	46	51
3. Loans per year	3.92	4.10	4.10	7.93	7.93	7.16
4. Annual total, adjusted for ave. maturity (line 1/line 3)	81.8	96.2	100.93	224.3[c]	249.8[c]	277.4[c]
5. Line 4 in constant (1982) dollars	121.5	133.2	128.4	191.1	205.9	219.6
6. Line 5 relative to 1977	100.0	109.6	105.7	157.3	169.5	180.7

[a]Figures for 1987, 1988, and 1989 are adjusted for the over-counting of overnight loans embodied in preceding line of table.
[b]From Column 1, Table 3.3.
[c]Figures for years 1987-1989 also affected by Note a.

Sources: Quarterly survey reports of STBL; and Table 3.3 above.

Average Size per Short-Term Business Loan
(thousands of dollars)

	1985	1989
a. One month and under	434	745
b. Over 1 month, less than 1 year	68	134
c. Demand loan	174	246

The Missing Link

Preceding pages have been preoccupied with examining why such a wide divergence exists between the general trend of the series on C + I loans outstanding at commercial banks, on one hand, and the trend shown in the data on new C + I loan creation, on the other. Generally speaking, there is no reason to expect a precise convergence between the growth rates of a stock series and a flow series. No exact convergence was presumed in the present instance either; but the discrepancy is such as to yield two differing indications of the state of the business-loan market. The immediately preceding pages, therefore, scrutinized in more detail the composition and methodology of the new-loan series. Even when certain adjustments or refinements were introduced, the fairly robust nature of the series was confirmed. In the following paragraphs, similarly, we extend the re-examination to the loans-outstanding data.

A large part of the discrepancy stems from the practice of marketization. In a world in which a banking house extended credit to industrial firms and held the loans thus made until their maturities, a fairly close correspondence would be observed between the growth of its loan portfolio and the pace of new lending, given no major change in the average maturity. This was indeed the traditional practice in the U.S. banking industry through most of its history. As banking firms grew in size and corporate complexity following World War II, the larger banks sold some business loans to their own nonbank affiliates. The loans thus sold were itemized in the aggregate reports for the industry in the 1970s, but amounted to less than two percent of total C + I loans outstanding.[7] Observation that in recent years there has been a tendency for the banking system's total holdings of C + I loans to grow at a slower rate than its creation of new loans suggests the possibility that banks are now retaining to maturity a smaller portion than formerly of the loans that they originate. Specifically, this prompts an examination of information about the extent of sales by banks from their portfolio of commercial and industrial loans.

As will appear from data to be presented below, banks have increasingly engaged, in the 1980s, in selling C + I loans to both bank and nonbank purchasers. While the statistics relating to these transactions do not take the form of series as lengthy or periodic as most banking data, and in some instances are constructed in a form making them difficult to compare with either the standard stock or flow statistics, they nevertheless are strongly indicative of a significant and, at this writing, still-rising volume of loan sales. Up to this time, the limited literature on this subject has been preoccupied mainly with microeconomic factors that motivate the individual bank to dispose of some of its loans, such as (depending on individual circumstances) the desire to diversify the industrial distribution of its portfolio, protect against interest-rate risk, or smooth the maturity profile, etc. The emphasis has tended to be upon profitability and risk-avoidance; and the practice of selling loans is viewed as related to the larger phenomenon of securitization.[8] By contrast, the focus in the present study is upon the effect of loan sales on the measurement of aggregate bank lending to business firms and the ability of balance-sheet data on C + I loans outstanding to serve as a measure of the absolute and relative volume of commercial-bank lending to that field.

One source pertinent to this subject is the information that has recently been collected by the regulatory authorities on the Consolidated Report of Condition. One of the schedules to that form now asks the respondent bank for the amount of "loans originated by the reporting bank that have been sold or participated to others during the calendar quarter ending with the report date," excluding portions retained by the reporting bank.[9] The instructions call for reporting loans originated by the reporter that were sold during the quarter, regardless of when they had been originated by the reporting bank. The resulting number for a given quarter thus constitutes the total gross *flow* of loan-sale transactions occurring during that quarter to all purchasers (specifically including the respondent's nonbank affiliates). As to type of loan covered, the reports apparently include loans of both short- and long-term maturities. Excluded are mortgage loans on 1-4 family residential properties; consumer loans; simple rollovers of loans previously sold by the reporter; loans sold under one-day repurchase agreements, and those transferred with recourse. Taking account of these excepted types, the data do include commercial and industrial loans, but also several other types that are *not* under study here--notably, those on nonresidential real estate, as well as agricultural, securities, and local government loans.

In view of the differences in their correspondence to the field under study here, the data on bank loans sold collected in the report of condition can not serve to displace the series on C + I loans outstanding, or to contribute specific modifications to that series. On the other hand, they have some impressionistic value. For the five years 1985-1989, the condition reports show that in the fourth quarter of those years the volume of loans sold by commercial banks with foreign operations rose from over $65 billion in 1985 to $272 billion and $243 billion in the last quarter of 1988 and 1989, respectively. Domestic banks without foreign operations recorded a smaller percentage increase, from about $10 billion in 1985 to almost $16 billion in 1989 (see Table 3.5). The figures quoted refer to sales to all purchasers.

Commencing with 1987, however, the condition report similarly called for data on loans purchased (defined in the same manner as for sales) in the quarter. In the three years 1987-1989, banks with foreign operations--typically large institutions--reported having bought only a small quantity of loans, an amount only 4 to 6 percent of the quantity they sold. For the domestic banks without foreign operations, on the other hand, purchased loans were almost one-half as large as the volume of those they sold, thus confirming that the smaller domestic banks are among the buyers of loans marketed by the large houses.

Moreover, the instigation of reporting on total loans purchased makes possible a calculation germane to our interest here--though too inclusive to be as pertinent a measure as we may find from another source. The two columns in Table 3.5 on loans purchased show, for each date, the total amount of loans made by commercial banks that had been purchased by (other) commercial banks during the quarter ending with the given date. In other words, the figures just referred to record the

TABLE 3.5 Selected Types of Loans Originated (Regardless of Date) by Reporting Bank That Had Been Sold During Given Quarter, 1985-1989 (millions of dollars)

| | Banks With Foreign Operations | | Banks Without Foreign Operations | |
	Loans Sold	Loans Purchased	Loans Sold	Loans Purchased
31 December 1985	65,742	--	9,998	--
31 December 1986	97,775	--	14,003	--
31 December 1987	183,562	10,709[a]	14,685	5,429[a]
31 December 1988	271,824	12,192	15,786	7,097
31 December 1989	243,101	13,027	15,837	7,113

[a]Beginning of series.

Sources: Table 5 of Report of Condition of Insured Commercial Banks, Call Aggregation Tables. Federal Deposit Insurance Corporation, various quarterly dates.

amount of bank loans of the types covered in the above-mentioned instructions that constituted loan-sales transactions withinthe U.S. domestic banking system (and that, therefore, did not affect the aggregate amount of outstanding loans of those types in the system). If the amount of loans purchased by banks in a given quarter is subtracted from the corresponding figure on loans sold to all purchasers for that quarter, the difference represents the volume of such loans sold to nonbank buyers, reducing the aggregate amount of outstanding loans in the banking system. In some instances, new loans, by prearrangement, are sold immediately to a purchaser without entering the originating bank's books.

Be it remembered that the condition report statistics just discussed above cover several other types of loan in addition to C + I loans, and it is possible that those other types together account for a sizable portion of the loans sold. Fortunately, a different set of data, dealing with sales of C + I loans only, has become available. Although this source has some limitations of its own, it provides a much more focused measurement for present purposes. In the late 1980s, through its standing contacts with senior loan officers at banks, the Federal Reserve carried out several Lending Practices Surveys (LPS) at roughly annual intervals on the subject of sales and participations of commercial and industrial loans. In addition to some nonstatistical information, the surveys have gathered data from an apparently well-selected panel of 60 respondent banks that are active market participants in loan sales and that, by reference to call report data, were found by the Board staff to account for more than 90 percent of gross loans sold (including C + I loans) by all banks in the second quarter of 1989. The respondents are instructed to report the total amount of C + I loans (all maturities) originated by them that they had sold or participated without recourse and that were still outstanding as of the survey date. Reporters also provided a distribution of the sales by type of purchaser. It is customary practice for the selling bank to continue to "service" the loan, receiving the interest payments but passing them through to the purchaser until maturity. Given this practice and the nature of the survey instructions, the data reported represent the total amount of C + I loans that, as of the specified date, had been sold by the originating bank and were still outstanding, without regard to date of origination or of maturity (see Table 3.6). The author is not aware of any estimate of the maturity distribution of loans that banks sell. That is not relevant to the questions addressed in these paragraphs, however, which are mainly concerned with who are the purchasers of the loans sold and whether the volume sold to nonbank buyers jeopardizes the reliability of series on loans outstanding at banks as a measure of commercial bank activity in providing credit to business.

A strongly rising volume of sales of C + I loans by the originating banks is apparent in the five LPS survey reports from the end of 1985 through June 30, 1990, as collated in Table 3.6. Respondents reported having outstanding sold loans of $26 billion in the first of those surveys and $80 billion in the last, an increase of 3.15 times. Over roughly the same time span, the total volume of loan sales of the *several* types covered by the condition-report data presented earlier in Table 3.5 showed an increase somewhat greater, of 3.74 times. The figures on C + I loan sales also roughly confirm the finding of Table 3.5 on the major share of large-

TABLE 3.6 Outstanding C + I Loans Sold or Participated to Others by Survey Respondents, 1985-1990
(billions of dollars)

By Purchaser	All LPS Respondents				All Respondents 06/30/90	Nine Money Center Banks 06/30/90	Other Banks 06/30/90
	12/31/85	03/31/87	06/30/88	06/30/89			
All purchasers	26.1	38.7	53.1	72.2	80.2	55.5	24.7
Large domestic banks	9.5	10.7	14.2	22.2	20.7	6.8	13.9
Other domestic banks	3.3	2.7	3.2	2.4	9.4	7.8	1.6
Buyers Other Than Domestic Banks:							
Branches and agencies of foreign banks	/11.7	14.8	16.7	30.1	26.1	19.4	6.7
Foreign offices of foreign banks	\	N.A.	6.9	2.5	4.7	4.1	0.6
Nonfinancial corporations	N.A.	1.9	3.2	4.8	6.3	5.7	0.6
All other	1.6	6.7	9.0	9.9	13.0	11.6	1.4
Total of lines 4-7: in dollars	13.3	23.4	35.8	47.3	50.1	40.5	9.3
as percentage of all loans sold:	51%	60%	67%	66%	63%	73%	38%

Sources: From data collected in periodic survey of Bank Lending Practices (LPS) by Board of Governors.

size banks in the loan-sales market. In the report for June 30, 1990, 69 percent of all C + I loans marketed were accounted for by nine money-center banks.

Of particular interest is the information revealed on the destination of the C + I loans that commercial banks have sold. Total sales as well as sales to buyers outside the banking field were already known by the Federal Reserve, in a general way, to be growing before the systematic LPS surveys in their present form were developed. The inauguration of periodic reporting began in time to confirm these impressions and to follow the rising trend over the past five years. On December 31, 1985, the portion of C + I loan sales bought by purchasers outside the field of domestically chartered and insured banks was already 51 percent of the total. The corresponding share in 1988 and 1989 was two-thirds of the total sold, followed by a slight dip in June 1990 to 63 percent, or $50 billion.

The purchasers other than domestic U.S. banks constitute two different sorts of institutions: (a) U.S. branches and agencies of foreign banks, and their home offices abroad; and (b) nonfinancial corporations, and "all other." (The all-other group includes thrift institutions, insurance companies, mutual funds, etc.) Among the foreign-related category, the greater part of the bank-loan buying was done by the U.S. branches and agencies, rather than the parent companies, which is also the case with the loans to U.S. business firms *originated* by foreign banks.

By utilizing the information on destinations of C + I loans sold by their originating banks, as contained in Table 3.6, it is possible to make certain illustrative adjustments to the data on business loans outstanding at commercial banks and competing lenders (Table 3.1). The object of this exercise is to reconstruct, so far as the data enable one to do, what the situation would be if all loans made to business firms continued to be held until. maturity by the lenders that had originated them. Accordingly, a partial remodeling of the data in Table 3.1 on loans outstanding was undertaken for the end of June 1989 and appears in the short Table 3.7. The $47.3 billion of C + I loans that had been sold by domestic banks to buyers other than domestic banks and that was still outstanding on June 30, 1989, was added to the published figure of $511.3 billion on the domestic banks' holdings of C + I loans on June 28 (last Wednesday series). Also from the same Table 3.6 data, the $30.1 billion of outstanding C + I bank loans that was reported as having been purchased by U.S. branches and agencies of foreign banks was subtracted from the figure on their holdings of those loans of $116.7 billion. No other adjustments similar to the preceding ones can be made for the remaining amount (of $17.2 billion) from the $47.3 billion that banks had sold to buyers outside the domestic banking system, owing to the lack of correspondence in classifications between the two data sources. The partial reconstruction of the end-June 1989 outstandings achieved by the two above adjustments produces the result of raising the domestic banks' share of the total by 4.5 percentage points and lowering that of the U.S. offices of foreign banks by 4.1 points, a net change totaling 8.6 percentage points.

Of the components that can not be satisfactorily accounted for at present in the relationship between the reported volume of business loans originated and the volume of those loans outstanding at banks, only one is of possible, but uncertain, significance. This concerns the quantity, if any, of commercial loans issued by foreign-related banks in the U.S. that may have been sold to domestic banks. Data on this subject appear to be unavailable at this time.[10]

Having examined at some length the construction and characteristics of the two main time series available for measuring the course of commercial and industrial loan volume, one arrives at the conclusion that for use in conjunction with data concerning the rate of interest on C + I loans the preferable statistics are those on the volume of new loans made, as collected by the Survey of Terms of Lending. That is the volume series of choice partly in order to avoid the distortions in the loans-outstanding numbers stemming from the large but not completely accountable quantity of loan sales and participations just examined above, but partly also for two additional reasons. One is the advantage that inheres from the identity of coverage that is assured between the volume and the rate series, since both are collected in the same Federal Reserve survey. The other advantage is a related but different one, namely, that the STBL volume and rate series both have the same time reference and periodicity.

It is instructive to look at the dollar volume and the average rate of interest on C + I loans simultaneously, to observe how they relate to each other over the time span during which both sets are available. This is the period commencing with 1977, when the STBL began to collect information on the volume of new business loans in addition to their

TABLE 3.7 Approximate Adjustment of Business Loans Outstanding to Reflect C + I Loans Sold to Buyers Other Than Domestic Banks

	June 28, 1989[a] (as reported)		June 28, 1989[a] (adjusted)	
	$ Billion	Percent	$ Billion	Percent
All commercial banks	628.6	80.0	645.2	80.4
Domestic banks	511.3	65.1	558.6	69.6
Weekly reporting banks	313.4	39.9	N.A.	--
New York City	56.4	7.2	N.A.	--
Outside New York City	257.0	32.7	N.A.	--
Other domestic	197.9	25.2	N.A.	--
Foreign banks	116.7	14.9	86.6	10.8
FSLIC-insured thrifts	32.5[b]	4.1	32.5[b]	4.1
Commercial paper, nonfinancial issuers	124.7	15.9	124.7	15.5
Total business credit	785.8	100.0	802.4	100.0
(Loans sold, not accounted for)			-16.6	
Memo:				
Commercial paper, financial issuers	378.7		378.7	

[a]Dollar figures on lines 1-7 are for last Wednesday in month, June 28. Lines 8 and 9, as well as adjustments derived from Table 3.6, refer to last day of month.
[b]Estimated.
  N.A.: Not available.

Sources: Lines 1-7 and line 9: Monthly tables in Federal Reserve Bulletin; line 8: estimated from Combined Financial Statements, Office of Thrift Supervision, 1989. Adjustments in column 3: from Table 3.6.

average rates. Use of the STBL data also permits us to concentrate on business loans of less than one year (which are not shown separately in the balance sheet data); and it is the short-term instrument that is the main subject under study.

Figure 3.2 presents quarterly statistics on the weighted-average interest rate and the total dollar volume of short-term C + I loans made at domestic commercial banks from 1977 to the present. For the first five years, both curves were rising strongly, with the interest rate climbing more steeply and somewhat leading the volume curve upward. While the lending rate reached its highest point in the third quarter of 1981, the upswing in the new loan volume did not peak until early 1983. After both variables had spurted upward again in 1984, they followed different paths for the rest of the 1980s. The interest rate drifted lower in 1985-1986, but then reversed directions and, except for a brief time in late 1986 and first quarter of 1987, stayed above and usually well above 8 percent for the rest of the decade. In contrast, the quantity of business loans in the second half of the 1980s continued to rise jerkily in current dollar terms, though only slowly in constant dollars.

The set of figures on the volume of new loans issued in the various survey weeks constitutes a sequence of total transactions in the market for business loans. The path traced by this series of loan transactions was influenced, of course, by many demand and supply factors affecting the borrowing corporations and the banks as lenders. Loan volume measured in constant dollars showed a near-continuous growth, but at varying rates of increase. It is difficult to find, in this fluctuating but generally-upward movement of borrowing-and-lending operations, a satisfactory explanation for the different behavior in the level and movement of the interest-rate curve. Correlation coefficients calculated for these data were well below the significant level.

Recapitulation

Lending by U.S. commercial banks to business firms grew steadily over the last 20 years, as measured by the volume of C + I loans outstanding. From 1977 through 1989, the average volume of business loans outstanding rose from $199 billion to $510 billion, an increase of 36 percent in real (1982 dollar) terms.

Outstanding loans to business firms by investors in commercial paper increased during this period at a more rapid rate than at commercial banks, though that growth rate was much more irregular. The volume of such paper at the end of 1989 was about 24 percent of that at banks.

FIGURE 3.2 Interest Rates and Volume of Business Loans Made at Commercial Banks

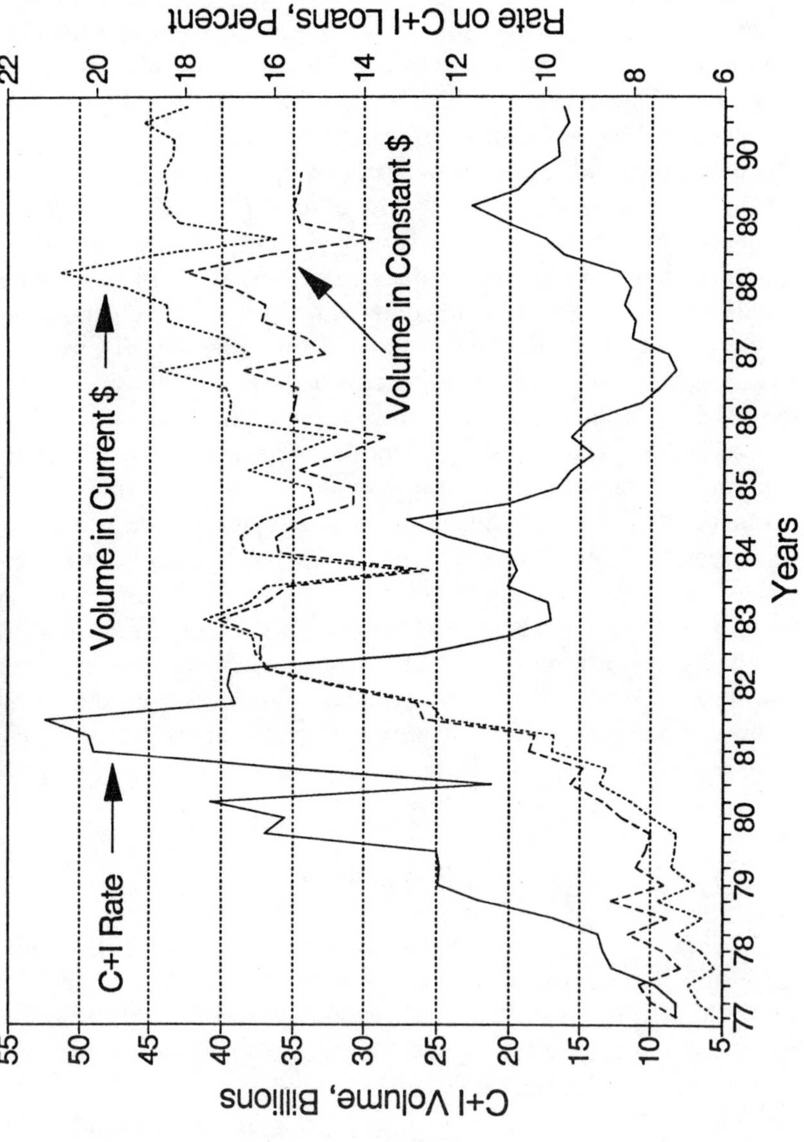

When all suppliers of credit to the business loan market are considered as a group, data on loan holdings outstanding show that the share of domestic commercial banks, though still by far the largest, has declined relatively since 1977 (especially for large New York City banks). Some analysts accept this as an accurate measurement of the comparative status of banks in the business loan market.

Data on the gross amount of new C + I loans originated by banks, by contrast, indicate a more vigorous growth of bank lending than do the figures on outstandings in bank portfolios. A large part of the discrepancy is explained by a marked rise in the sale of loans by the originating banks to purchasers *outside* the (domestic) banking system. Those loan sales and participations are occurring largely in response to the respective interests and choices of both buyers and sellers, and do not necessarily indicate an equivalent "deterioration" in the banks' status in the business-loan market.

One can arrive at the tentative judgment that, whatever may be the factors explaining the heightened level and fluctuation of interest rates on business loans, they do not appear to have stemmed from secular change in the annual volume, absolute or relative, of loan transactions originated.

Moreover, when the respective movements in volume and interest rate of new short-term C + I loans are compared on a quarterly basis, for the period since 1977, there is no discernible uniform correlation, statistical or graphic, in their behavior. It remains to be seen whether an adequate explanation for this short-term rate can be found by reference to phenomena outside these price-quantity confines of the business-loan market itself.

Notes

1. For further discussion on the origin, functioning, and dismantling of these deposit-rate ceilings, see Young 1973: pp. 155-159; Cargill and Garcia 1985: chap. 5; Litan 1987: pp. 32-35; Brown 1987: pp. 1-11; Mayer et al. 1981: chap. 8.

2. Prior to July 1959, commercial bank loans made to financial institutions were not shown separately. Some loans to financial institutions had been included in C + I loans, and some each in two other groups. Board of Governors 1976: pp. 149-150.

3. Useful analyses of the commercial paper market are Meek 1982: pp. 83-86; Cook and Rowe 1986: pp. 111-125; Meulendyke 1990: pp. 98-100.

4. The term nonfinancial issuers "includes public utilities and firms engaged primarily in such activities as communications, construction, manufacturing, mining, wholesale and retail trade, transportation, and services." *Federal Reserve Bulletin*, September 1990, Table 1.32, p. A23.

5. Estrella 1986: pp. 160-163; Cook and Rowe 1986: pp. 120-121. Litan 1987: pp. 42-43 is somewhat ambivalent on whether to include finance company issuance of commercial paper with that of nonfinancial business firms.

6. E.g., Estrella, p. 174; Litan, pp. 42-45.

7. Board of Governors 1981: Table 15, pp. 74-80, and p. 573.

8. Pavel and Phillis 1987; Pavel 1986; Laub 1988; Cumming 1987. It should be noted that, with regard to the increased volume of (business) loan sales, some observers find it intriguing to project the continued, if not limitless, extension of this practice. That envisages an ultimate situation in which some commercial banks would be only originators of, say, C + I loans, while others would be purchasers; some banks would specialize in creating one type of loan, other banks in a different type, etc., while secondary markets for each type would develop through loan sales or securitizing. At the logical limit, loan-creating banks would hold no portfolio of loans and would receive no loan interest income, with the latter replaced by origination fees. The articles referred to acknowledge certain inhibitions caused by a bank's desire to retain a continuing customer relationship; and perceive that C + I loans are more heterogeneous than mortgage or consumer loans, and hence more difficult to securitize in packages.

9. Language quoted is from memoranda section of Schedule RC-L of report form FFIEC 031, Consolidated Report of Condition for Insured Commercial and State-Chartered Savings Banks for June 30, 1990. The instructions to the form were also consulted.

10. For the purpose at hand, the foreign banks constitute the only other source of short-term lending to business firms that could be statistically significant. Commercial loan holdings at savings and loan firms are relatively small in total, and declining. As for commercial paper issued by nonfinancial borrowers, the literature on this market is clear that sales of outstanding paper are negligible and that a secondary market does not exist for these note instruments. See Cook and Rowe, pp. 117-118.

4

The Theory of Interest in Economics

> I know your opinion of the political economy of the day: I have
> a better opinion of it than you have; but, if I write anything on the
> subject, it will be never losing out of sight the purely provisional
> character of all its concrete conclusions.
>
> ---John Stuart Mill, in letter to
>
> Auguste Comte (1844)

If the length of time that has elapsed since a given economic
subject first appeared in the writings of learned men were a gauge of
the solidity of thought about its nature and functioning, then one of
the most securely solid branches of economics would be the theory of
interest and the interest rate. The chronicle could include both passing
references and much longer treatments of the subject that stretch from
Ancient Greece to the current moment.

Contemporary economists rightly hold that most of the views
expressed about interest before 1800 are rude and illogical and have
been superseded. The fact remains that the payment of interest
between borrower and lender attracted the attention of a long
succession of writers whose ranks include philosophers, historians, the
medieval Schoolmen, political and social scientists, and legislators.
Some of them were expositors seeking mainly to describe the practices
of economic life of an exciting epoch, such as the period of emerging
capitalism of the Renaissance. While some ancient writers were
fascinated by what they observed, most were repelled or abhorrent of
a practice they saw as unjust or which they tried to judge by
ecclesiastical law.

Virtually all citations prior to the latter part of the eighteenth
century were indeed scattered references incidental to the subject of

money-lending---usually judgemental in character---and lacking the benefit of being incorporated in any comprehensive body of general economic theory such as was to come in later years. It is not the intent of this book to detail the entire history of economic thought concerning interest. The object of this chapter will rather be to review or summarize the main lines of approach to the subject of interest that either are generally accepted or that have been active elements of professional discussion.

Before proceeding to examine the main types of current economic theory on interest just referred to, one finds it instructive to hark back briefly to what the truly ancient thinkers found absorbing and important with regard to interest. This brief exercise will reveal some similarities, as well as many obvious differences, between that long medieval period and the present time---both in theoretical doctrine and in observed market practice.

The Medieval Position Regarding Interest

Although it is convenient to adopt the label "medieval position" as a shorthand expression, the beliefs and behavior referred to actually displayed a persistent character over a historical span extending from about the end of the Roman empire through the fifteenth century--- more than 1000 years, with a degree of fuzziness at both ends. Use of the term "medieval" is also justified by the fact that it was in this age that the subject received the greatest amount of clerical and secular attention and that the strictures of those ecclesiastical writers known as the Schoolmen became codified in Canon Law. In substantive content, the canonists did not advance much beyond Aristotle's position much earlier, though their texts were prolix.

What the views regarding interest-taking consisted of was a doctrine that was negative, censorious, and severe. The prohibition represented the religious and moral philosophy of the Church; the taking of interest was forbidden, as a sin, and was binding on the faithful. Those who violated the prohibition faced the risks of dying as a sinner, being refused a Christian burial, and punishment in the life to come. In arriving at this prohibition, the canonists cited various reasons or sources of authority. One of these was the much earlier and similar injunction against interest-taking that appeared plainly in at least two passages of the Bible, in which the Hebrews were forbidden to exact interest in lending money. The prohibition applied to loans "to any of my people" or, differently phrased, "to thy brother", just as the medieval canonists applied their doctrine only to members of *their* own faith. While this biblical precedent had been only explained on vague grounds of tribal brotherhood, the medieval scholars also leaned heavily on the philosophic authority of Aristotle, whose censure of interest was argued on theoretical reasoning.

Athens, in the fourth century B.C., was a functioning money economy (as was the land of Israel, to a degree, in the prophets' day), and Aristotle explicitly recognized the roles of money as a medium of exchange, store of value, and unit of account. His economic views did not extend into theories on value and distribution. He argued that money is meant to serve as a medium for exchange of goods, but it is barren (as compared with cattle or land or labor), and since money does not yield a product one cannot charge for its use. Moreover, canonists also declared that usury[1] flaunted the biblical commands of brotherly love and justice, and thus was antisocial.

The doctrine of the Church on interest that was formulated in medieval times showed great longevity, in broad principle. It was tolerated by local and other governmental authorities, and in some cases adopted in civil law. In the atomistic and weak political units that prevailed for a long period after the disintegration of the Roman empire, the prohibition of interest was compatible with other aspects of feudal regulation of vocational and commercial matters. Not only were the secular bodies content to let the Church take the lead on a prohibition that irked lenders and borrowers, but the Church as an institution had become the largest economic agent and a political power able to assert its position. In its dual role, it tended to look at economic instruments and activities from a viewpoint that combined commercial considerations with preachments to society on justice, love, and charity. Here, too, the Schoolmen found theoretical support in the writing of Aristotle, whose relatively limited comments on financial matters were contained in works that bore the titles of *Politics* and *Ethics* and that stressed moral constraints which would characterize the ideal city-state he projected.

In the later Middle Ages, improvements in navigation and the growth of cities were accompanied by an expansion of local and interregional commerce, with a corresponding need for financial instruments and products. Even in the preceding period, the willingness of lenders to forgo charging interest on loans had been reluctant, and resulted in evasions. In addition to simple non-compliance with the prohibition, moreover, steps were taken to accommodate the demand for a dependable loan market that was not clandestine and illegal. One such development that came later and irregularly was that some cities or regions adopted regulations permitting some types of loan to bear interest, but subject to a given maximum rate. Parallel and even preceding that, however, was the recognition by the clerical authorities themselves of some given circumstance that would justify an exception to the prohibition. As one example, if a loan was not repaid on the date specified in the contract, a "penalty" of a specified amount could be payable; or, instead of making an overt loan agreement, lender and borrower would write a temporary "partnership", with the eventual payment to the party supplying the money to be called the income from his investment in the partnership. The ingenuity displayed by bankers and other money-lenders during the twelfth to fourteenth centuries in devising financial innovations for their borrowers flowered so luxuriantly that one economic historian was able to list ten different types which, also with some sub-species, were able to qualify for exception to the usury prohibition.[2]

By the eighteenth century, the sanction against interest on loans was so riddled with exceptions and weakened by non-enforcement that it was almost inoperative in most industrial countries. This erosion process had been hastened in some countries by the Reformation, with the Calvinists early taking the view that interest payment was a practice that encouraged thrift and industriousness in society and promoted a productive capitalist economy. The Catholic authorities, while ceasing to enforce their doctrine, did not formally revoke it until the twentieth century. National and provincial governments maintained or enacted interest controls at various times, in the form of maximum lending rates applicable to certain types of loans. In most instances, this sort of re-defined usury prohibition has also been abolished in modern times.[3]

Rationale and Economic Impact

At any point in history, the position taken by the authorities in power with regard to the financial market is likely to reflect a combination of elements: theoretical beliefs and dogma, institutional arrangements, and policy considerations. If one makes allowance for differences in the overall state of economic development in medieval times as compared with our own, those same elements are found operating in both periods. The nation-states that were to emerge as part of the Renaissance process had not yet been formed, and the numerous principalities and duchies across the face of Europe were preoccupied by rivalries and weakened by wars.

In the economic sphere, this decentralization of political authority did not imply a complete absence of economic power and control, but led rather to a tacit division of that power---to the extent that it seemed necessary to exercise it---between ecclesiastical and secular bodies. All land, with the significant exception of the vast holdings of the monasteries, abbeys, and other religious establishments, belonged in principle to the prince or duke and to the vassals upon whom they conferred delegated rights. The hierarchical system of mutual rights and obligations between socio-economic layers served to handle most matters of taxes and revenues. Since many of these obligations were specified in terms of given quantities of grain or hours of labor, they could be fulfilled in kind, rather than by cash transactions. The feudal system can be regarded as its method of dealing with the timeless economic problem, scarcity, by a medieval form of "incomes policy" applicable to wages and commodity prices and also to interest rates. Most cash payments were effected in metal coin, and it was an accepted fact that the coinage of money was the right and duty of the sovereign or his designated officer.

No country had a national monetary authority, in the form of the modern central bank with broad discretionary powers to influence the terms of money and credit. The first such institution was not founded until the seventeenth century. Nevertheless, the medieval sovereign affected (knowingly or not) the quantity and value of money in the realm in several ways, through: (a) changing the volume of public expenditures; (b) reducing or increasing the amount of money of a given specification minted and expended; (c) altering the metallic content per coin minted; and (d) borrowing from money-lenders. If loans to the prince did not already enjoy an exception to the Church's interest prohibition, he could turn to the Jewish money-lenders, who were not addressed by Canon Law.

In sum, the market *practice* of money-lending at interest in the early Middle Ages was restricted by the operation of the religious ban on interest-taking. But the limitation of total credit volume produced thereby probably was not great, owing to the slow pace of economic development as well as to the widespread practice of lending and repayment in kind; and the poor could get personal loans interest-free. In the *later* medieval times, the demand curve for commercial credit--- though we cannot draw it with precision---obviously had shifted markedly to the right. Presumptive evidence for this is found in the number and wide variety of commercial circumstances that were granted exemption from the interest prohibition. It can also be inferred from observing that in instances when the civil authorities took the legitimizing step of enacting a ceiling on the rate of interest that could be charged, that maximum was often set at a fairly moderate level of about 10 percent, which—as a fixed ceiling—does not suggest the probability of a scarcity of loanable funds sufficient to create a significant volume of unsatisfied demand for credit. Nevertheless, it seems quite likely that the negative climate and the steps necessary to qualify under the regulations may have favored to some degree the opting for direct investment and risk-taking participation by medieval and Renaissance entrepreneurs, as against credit-financed activity.[4]

To modern economists, the main focal point is centered on how interest rates are determined and how changes in their level relate to the behavior of other major variables in the economy. The medieval scholars' approach was much narrower and different. Having concluded that usury (i.e., interest-bearing lending) could not be justified on the logical basis that they formulated, they regarded it as contrary to their values. Their central values were those of justice, charity, individual rights that were real but subject to the common good, and a preoccupation with heavenly salvation rather than worldly goods. It was against this socio-moral background that the clerical scholars considered all economic matters; and when it came to money and the lending of it, they looked at it as a branch of trade. Trading was regarded as quite different from, and subordinate to, agriculture and manufacturing both of which involved an alteration of form by means of inputs of labor and materials. No such transforming or adding of factor inputs could, it was held, be claimed for trade in general; and some forms (such as retailing) were disdained especially.

Lowest of all in the medieval view was the trade of money-lending. Starting from the hypothetical example of a direct exchange of one good for another under a barter system, the canonists, following Aristotle, argued that exchange would occur only if the two articles had the same value. Any exchange that lacked this quality of equivalence would be unjust and "unnatural". Among other writers, Saint Thomas Aquinas declared that while human failings might lead some men to sell objects for more than their worth, this was contrary to God's will, and only transactions that assured joint advantage were just. Pursuant to this criterion, a transaction in which money was utilized in its neutral role of the means of payment was admissible, provided that the sale was executed at the "just price". (The medieval clerics, including Saint Thomas, failed to produce an objective definition or method of deriving the just price, and in usage it tended to be taken as meaning the going price conventionally recognized in guild or other market circles.

In applying this chain of reasoning about trade to *loans* denominated in money, the prevailing theory looked askance at all lending transactions as unproductive and "unnatural". Money, as the circulating medium provided (exogenously, to use a very post-medieval term) by the sovereign at no direct cost to the lender, was deemed infertile and unproductive and thus incapable of performing other than a transitional function. In general, therefore, the lender should not expect to receive any compensation beyond the repayment of the sum borrowed.

Parallels and Modern Previews

The alert reader may note, in passing, a slight resemblance between this distinction made many centuries ago between money and goods and the twentieth-century differentiation between money and other financial assets. Specifically, the reader will note that one of the attributes that economists and the banking authorities have recognized as characterizing the components of the U.S. money stock, as narrowly defined (M1), is that these components[5] are accepted throughout the economy as a means of payment without discount or interest charge. The analogy is only partial, of course. It is mentioned only to emphasize that even in the inchoative state of economic thought that characterized the scholarly writing of pre-Renaissance Europe there was an intuitive perception, however incipient and imperfect, of the distinct nature of money and its roles.

Another example that is a closer anticipation of a contemporary theoretical concept can be observed in one type of exception made to the Church's prohibition of interest-taking loans. This hypothetical situation was that of an investor and lender who also conducted business activities for his own account. If he should agree to lend money to a merchant or other commercial borrower, he would be forgoing the ability to employ the sum in question to produce income in his own projects. After pondering this situation over a considerable period, the clerical authorities evolved a doctrine concerning this *lucrum cessans*.[6] They held that in cases where the loan of money caused the lender to lose the opportunity of gainfully employing his funds elsewhere, this sacrifice justified the exaction of interest on the loan. To this author's knowledge, the decision conceding this (or any other exemption) presumably was confined to stating the principle involved, and left the rate of interest for the parties to fix. In logic, only the lender himself, in a given case, would know *which* alternative investment he was forgoing and its estimated return.

The principle embodied in the argument that a lost or escaped chance for gain represents an economic cost was re-discovered in the latter part of the nineteenth century. First to write about it was Austrian economist Friedrich von Wieser, and the concept quickly entered into the professional lexicon as the "opportunity-cost" principle. Its timely arrival on the scene gave further ammunition to the Austrian and British marginalists, including Alfred Marshall, who were contending that subjective demand factors as well as supply factors jointly determine market prices. As formulated by Buchanan, "The concept of opportunity cost...expresses the basic relationship between scarcity and choice...Opportunity cost is the evaluation placed on the most highly-valued of the rejected alternatives or opportunities".[7] As the breadth of this definition implies, the concept is a tool employed in a wide variety of analytical situations in economics that involve choices by sellers or buyers with regard to their production or purchasing or marketing alternatives---and in the monetary field, with regard to holding or offering alternative forms of financial assets.[8]

Indeed, a closing word about the medieval writers can be that, although they did not explicitly enunciate a theory of the determination of the price (interest rate) of loans, their embryonic concept of opportunity cost appears to identify what the asking price of the lender would be: i.e., it would be not less than the rate of return on the most lucrative of the rejected alternative investment options. Note that, as recent opportunity cost theory recognizes, the individual lender's perception of his preferred alternative need not be identical either with that of other market participants or, *a fortiori*, with the resulting market rate.

Classical Beginnings: Capital-Related Loans

In the ancient world and in the long medieval period that faded away only as the renascent forces in Europe gradually became dominant in the 15th and 16th centuries, whatever scholarly attention was devoted to the subject of interest was condemnatory and, in principle, prohibitive. As we saw in the preceding section, the attitude displayed by the powerful church authorities toward interest-taking by lenders was serious-minded and far from casual. But it was essentially the approach of a prosecuting attorney preparing a brief to interpret and apply a juridical position already established, rather than that of an unbiased researcher seeking objectively to analyze facts and economic processes.

The hostile element in the medieval opposition to interest-bearing loans is explicable not only in terms of ecclesiastical doctrine, a major part of which was an injunction to be charitable and protective toward the poorer members of society, and which assumed that a large share of potential borrowers were the needy. It also reflected the social climate and institutional framework of a continent that had been fragmented, the parts of which had become isolationist if not wholly isolated, and that tended to cope with the economic problem of scarcity in a conserving fashion, by myriad rules or structures to prevent a further decline. The gradually-emerging fact that (apart from consumer loans) the demand for loans was destined largely for financing external trade or expanding the incipient manufacturing arts seemed to menace the existing predominantly agrarian socio-economic structure.

Those restrictive, conservationist forces, however, whether originating in religious doctrine or feudal social patterns, were fighting a losing battle. By the closing years of the eighteenth century, the processes of social and economic development had produced in the major nation-states such changes in the industrial structure and the patterns of domestic employment and foreign trade that, in consequence, writers appeared with a livelier, broader interest in trying to explain economic phenomena in a more systematic and integrated manner. These writers in the field of "political economy", who held sway from the turn into the nineteenth century until about 1870, would eventually become referred to as the "classical school" of economics. Since we seek to know what economic theory has to say about the determination and behavior of interest rates, our search must necessarily begin with classical economics and include a small number of subsequent schools of professional thought that grew out of, though did not necessarily supersede, the classical economic theory. In this survey of interest-rate theory, the exposition will gain in clarity and expedition if the pertinent views are presented mainly in terms of schools---groups who share a predominantly common position regarding interest---rather than of individual economists.[9]

While the classical economists devoted some attention to how pricing and production decisions were reached in a given firm or industry, they were still more absorbed in analyzing how the economy as a whole functions and grows. These early pioneers in macroeconomics were aware of flawed and one-sided schemes that had been advanced by writers in the preceding century---the mercantilists---on how a country could attain international dominance over its neighbors (by means, for example, of a discriminatory foreign trade policy). They adopted a broader approach, therefore, to inquire how the national product as a whole grows and the manner by which that national income and product comes to be divided among the economic factors or agents of production.

In addressing these questions, they proceeded from certain expressed or tacit assumptions. Taking for granted the existence (and, in the main, the beneficence) of the prevailing system of private capitalism, they identified the factors contributing to the productive process as being land, labor, and capital. The income produced, by a given industry or by the whole economy, was accordingly to be divided among the owners who had provided those three factors of production, in relation to the proportions employed, as determined by the current state of technological arts. Classical economists assumed that open competition as well as full employment prevailed, and that technical knowledge was wide-spread. Given these assumptions, they developed separate theories governing the distribution of income among the three shares, with particular reference to agriculture. They held that land, since it was not reproducible, could command rent because of its innate scarcity, the rental amount varying according to the respective location and fertility. As for labor's share, the accepted wage theory was that the population was indeed growing over time--- which the classicists acknowledged---but that its rate of growth was limited by the available quantity of the "means of subsistence", primarily the quantity of food. Therefore, the size of the labor force as well as the level of wages were regarded as known and substantially constant in the short run; and these amounts were determined in the long run by the pace of increase in the means of subsistence, which was deemed to be very slow. The remaining income share was termed "profit", and was paid to the entrepreneur. Although this share remaining for the owner was thus a residual, it was considered as embracing not only his reward for risk-taking and managerial input but also the payment or reimbursement to him for the use of his own or borrowed money. Thus interest was regarded as part of the "profits" share, whether or not its payment involved an explicit payment to others.[10]

Classical economics was conscious of the fact that the phenomenon of interest presented itself in two different forms: as an *aggregate* that constitutes a share in the total income of an industry or nation; and as a percentage or *ad valorem rate* that denotes, in decimal terms, the fractional price to be paid per annum for the use of one unit of the currency borrowed. Before proceeding on with the rate of interest, which is the main focus of this volume, one should note the fact that the question of what relationship existed between interest and profit was one which intrigued and agonized economic theorists from the early classical period well into the twentieth century.[11] Writers in the early period of political economy tended to regard the flow of interest as part of the profits share of distributed income, as stated above, with its volume varying with the amount of investment activity, and with the funds invested often originating partly from the investor-entrepreneur himself. Some held that the same economic factors affected both profits and interest, and to the same degree. Occasionally the two terms were used interchangeably.

Given the equilibrium conditions postulated in the classical framework, the price and volume available of the first two input factors, land and labor, were known and fixed. It therefore appeared to follow that borrowing for a potential investment project could and would always be undertaken if the expected future return on the required capital would be equal to or greater than the interest rate paid on the funds borrowed (or the imputed opportunity cost to the entrepreneur of using his own funds). This "natural" equilibrium rate of interest thus represented the cost incurred in giving up present real resources, which would be forgone for current consumption, in exchange for future resources. If the person providing the borrowed funds were someone other than the entrepreneur, this lender also, under the same conditions, would possess knowledge of the prices of land and labor as well as the prospective capital yield from prevailing technology; and would be willing to lend only at an interest rate at least equal to the expected physical return. In sum, the equilibrium rate of interest in the classical theory--while it would be paid in money terms--was in essence conceived in barter terms representing the physical productivity of capital. The money would serve as a means of payment but did not exercise a determining role in establishing the interest rate.

Fully recognizing that this equilibrium rate of interest was an abstraction, economists of the period regarded it as having analytical value, and they described it as the "natural" or "normal" or sometimes the "average" rate. Contrasted with this "natural" rate was the "market" or "money" rate, which referred to the actual interest charged at a given time on loan transactions, and which might be higher or lower than the natural rate for numerous reasons.[12]

In connection with the barter or non-monetary aspect of interest theory in classical economics, there are other aspects and implications that should be observed. This applies particularly to that part of the theory that embraces the concept of a "natural" rate of interest. It evolved from a body of thought in which the price of a good was said to be determined by the forces of "supply and demand"; but these forces had not yet been envisioned in terms of two schedules or continuous curves on a two-dimensional diagram. Classical value theory was essentially one in which price was governed by the costs of production incurred by the seller, which included interest. It was commonly accepted that all members of the society have a preference for present goods over future goods. Hence, a businessman would only be willing to commit his current efforts and resources to a project if the investment would improve his profits and the productive efficiency of his operations. That outcome was regarded, in the enthusiastic climate of the Industrial Revolution then prevailing, as most likely to be achieved through investment projects that added to the stock of physical capital. A saver would be willing to abstain from consuming a part of his income if the cost (sometimes even described as the pain) of his "abstinence" would be compensated by receiving an interest payment commensurate with the improved efficiency of output that his loan would facilitate. Thus the "natural" interest rate of classical theory represented the rate that would be determined for *long-term* capital-related loans, under the conditions of perfect competition assumed, at a given moment.

Although the natural rate was described as a loan price that was compatible with maintaining equilibrium in the commodities or goods markets, that did not necessarily mean the maintenance of a stationary state. Although not always so stated, the equilibrium rate could be affected by new conditions. The state of the technical arts was evolving, and the labor force was also growing, though the two were not rising at the same pace. In short, it would be incorrect to regard the classicists' natural rate as necessarily being a constant over time, even if it could be visualized (though not identified numerically *ex ante*) at a given moment. We can revert to this point later.

A more valid reproach to the concept of a natural rate of interest concerns the automaticity asserted in the manner of its determination. The entrepreneur who hired the other factors of production in a given enterprise was also the person who made decisions about whether to invest his own or borrowed funds in a given new project. Moreover, it was assumed that whenever the interest rate at lenders equaled a borrowing cost low enough to assure a competitive price on the finished product, the entrepreneur would always borrow. Similarly, the saver would always lend the required financing whenever the entrepreneur/borrower would meet his offering rate of interest. Not until many decades later did economic theory recognize that there could be, for more than a purely transitory period, some withholding of funds by potential lenders or some refraining from embarking on investment projects by entrepreneurs for reasons other than interest-rate considerations. Such a possibility, however, is and was always present in a money economy.[13] The framework of assumptions in classical interest-rate theory was too narrow to encompass a potential withholding as an *inherent* possibility.

From Classical to Neoclassical Economics

So far as interest-rate theory is concerned, the treatment by the neoclassical economists is a recognizable outgrowth of the views held in the preceding classical period. With the refinements and elaboration to be described below, this modified body of thought dominated economic thinking about interest rated from the 1870s on, and flourished virtually unchallenged until the 1930s. Not only was the period long in duration, but it was one in which the size of the economic profession was rapidly growing in all Western countries, and the scope of economic inquiry was expanding laterally. It is not surprising that the principal stream of classical theory pertaining to the rate of interest was, from time to time, joined by some tributary. Meandering away by offshoots was not important, moreover, and the confluence had become fairly broadly unified by the opening of the twentieth century.

The main doctrine on interest-rate determination that was received by late-19th/early 20th century economists from their predecessors, as described in the preceding section, was that the "natural" rate of interest was a phenomenon fundamentally related to the formation or expansion of capital. It was determined by the forces of demand and supply, between entrepreneur-investors and saver-lenders whose basis for bid and offer, at any given moment, was the expected physical return to be earned by the investment in question. The resulting capital loan was long-term, and was thought of as a barter transaction, though denominated and paid in the pertinent medium of exchange. The rate thus delineated was conceived as the loan rate that, under the specified conditions of full employment and perfect competition, would maintain economic equilibrium under those conditions and the given state of the technical arts. Interest rates prevailing in the market at a given date might well differ from that equilibrium rate, due to various circumstances and forces not conforming to the underlying economic forces embodied in the equilibrium rate itself.

Classical economics did not develop any systematic or general theory to explain market interest rates. Some writers did indeed sometimes comment on particular instances in which current market rates had risen or fallen markedly, but the treatment tended to be of an *ad hoc* nature.

By the 1870s, professional economic theory had developed along several major lines of analysis to the extent that their respective findings could, with some adaption, be applied to the closer study of the determination and behavior of interest rates. For example, the presentation of value theory, dealing with how relative prices of individual goods are determined, had progressed beyond the simplistic labor-cost theory of value that underlay the classical explanation of the supply side of the microeconomic pricing process. Instead, the sellers in a firm or an industry were recognized as operating on the basis of a supply curve, showing the number of units that would be offered for sale at various prices, reflecting the marginal cost of producing the respective quantity. Similarly, the buyers' side of the market was portrayed by a demand curve that reflected, in its downward slope, the diminishing marginal utility, in monetary terms, of additional units of the good to the industrial or household consumers in that market. Thus the quantity that would be sold of the given good as well as the selling price were determined at the point at which the marginal cost curve intersected with the marginal demand or revenue curve, and this "utility theory of price" placed equal causal emphasis on demand and supply.

The earlier economists had presented an explanation of how, under simulated barter conditions, a quantity of physical capital today could be said to be lent in the loan (i.e., bond) market to an investor at a rate of interest corresponding to the expected rate of return, from the additional investment, in future goods. That concept of a loan transaction that was executed in physical terms, or at least describable in a capital-related analogy, was retained by their neoclassical followers, while recasting it in marginal productivity terms. They also retained the idea that the loan rate corresponding to the productivity rate was an equilibrium interest rate that would maintain but not increase the capital stock and the level of activity. But they were not comfortable to ignore the transactions occurring in the financial market at the actual, current market or money rate of interest. The question to be answered was, how did it relate to the "natural" rate?

The person who contributed most toward achieving a better synthesis of neoclassical developments in the field of production and capital formation with the field of monetary theory was Knut Wicksell. Although his interests and writings covered a broad range of general economic theory, including the economics of the individual firm, his main preoccupation was with macroeconomic fluctuations. In particular, Wicksell's studies were centered on finding explanations for why the general price level rises or falls. The answer he elaborated to that question involved setting forth a model describing an inter-relationship between the commodities markets and the financial markets that, while drawing on previous economic thought, was more complete. In this model, the main variables were the general price level, investment demand, aggregate domestic demand, the natural rate of interest, the market rate, and the money stock.

Wicksell's presentation, which appears in substantially the same description in many passages of his works, proceeds along the following lines. The rate of interest that is normal or "natural" is one corresponding to the return that would be earned on an investment of physical capital, under assumed conditions of perfect competition and full employment. As the classical school had said, the level of the natural rate as thus defined constitutes a *necessary* condition for maintaining the economy in equilibrium. But, declared Wicksell, it is not a *sufficient* condition: the additional required condition is that the market rate for capital loans must be equal to the "natural" rate if stability is to be maintained.[14] Equivalence between the two interest rates may occur at times, but it is far from characteristic, and they are more likely to differ than to coincide, it was said. Owing to the different forces that are constantly playing on the demand or supply of money in the financial markets, the market rate of interest can be above or below the natural rate. This stems from the two rates being determined independently and by different forces. A grasp of the natural rate "is obtained by thinking of it as the rate which would be determined by supply and demand if real capital goods were lent in kind without the intervention of money," and it was noted that the supply of real capital is clearly limited by physical conditions. By contrast, "the supply of money is in theory unlimited and even in practice is held within fairly elastic boundaries."[15]

Although disparities between the natural and the market rates were acknowledged to be not infrequent, the neoclassical economists nevertheless declared that any disparity tended to set in motion, automatically, equilibrating forces that would return the rates to equality and restore equilibrium. While such a self-stabilizing action might, to some, have seemed self-evident---i.e., subsumed within the overall framework of neoclassical belief in a general tendency toward long-run equilibrium---Wicksell constructed a specific description of the "cumulative process" that he believed acted to remove a discrepancy between the two rates. In his expositions of the process, it usually was set in motion by some exogenous event that caused the market interest rate to deviate from the natural rate (or widened a spread already existing), the standard example being a significant net injection of money into the system. If the money rate had been below (or now was pushed further below) the natural interest rate, entrepreneurs could profitably expand their borrowing and employ the funds to augment their purchases of investment goods; under the full-employment assumption, this newly-increased demand would raise prices of capital goods initially and of all goods ultimately. The inflationary gap in the commodities market would increase the volume of borrowing necessary in the capital market and thereby initiate upward pressure on interest rates, such that the market rate would soon be raised "to its normal level, so that it again coincides with the natural rate."[16]

In sum, an increase in the quantity of money in the system had the effect, under the assumed conditions, of lowering the market interest rate, increasing the volume of borrowing, raising the level of total demand and prices in the commodities markets. The market interest rate would then rise and again become equal to the natural rate, the demand for loans now having caught up with and reversed the original lowering of the supply price of loans. In the earlier and simpler formulations of the theory, the "cumulative process" was stated in terms of restoring an equilibrium at the original numerical level---i.e., the general case in which the original "natural" interest rate, as governing or independent variable, had not been affected.

Note that the classical and neoclassical schools---like the medieval Schoolmen before them, and on back in antiquity to Aristotle---regarded money as neutral insofar as having any governing effect on the equilibrium levels of macroeconomic factors is concerned. Within their system of static equilibrium thought, therefore, the Wicksellian cumulative adjustment process had its operational result only on the market rate of interest. In later writings, Wicksell recognized that exceptions or an alteration in basic economic factors could change the natural or "normal" rate to a new level; and also conceded readily that the market or money rate could continue to deviate from the natural one for protracted periods that did not yield promptly to the hypothesized automaticity of the ideal cumulative process.[17]

While the neoclassical treatment of interest rates was presented in the past few pages primarily in the formulation of Knut Wicksell, his views have been considered as representative of the school and as probably the most comprehensive and lucid in expository style.[18] On the basis of this review, we can begin to assess what professional economic theory, up through the writings of the neoclassical school, can contribute to an understanding of the determination and behavior of interest rates on short-term loans by commercial banks to business firms, which is the subject of this book.

One characteristic that is most apparent about neoclassical interest-rate analysis is that it is addressed invariably to "the" rate of interest, in the singular. It is equally clear that this usage is applied with reference to both the natural rate and the market rate. A different, though somewhat related, point is that the loan instrument under consideration by these economists in both markets is explicitly a capital loan (i.e., a bond or debenture). An occasional reference appears to "the structure of rates" in the market; but this turns out to refer only to different maturities (i.e., the term structure) of that one type, *the* long-term capital loan. While it is acceptable, of course, for simplicity of exposition to speak of *the* rate in the sense of some assumed, though unstated, representative or composite rate (such as a weighted average), this is nowhere explained, and even in the capital market there are bond rates that vary in level and other attributes among themselves.

The Wicksellian analysis devotes a considerable amount of attention to the importance it attaches to the relationship between two variables that it identifies as the natural rate of interest and the market or money rate. The theory asserts that for maintaining long-term equilibrium the two interest rates must be at the same level; and it describes the presumed consequential effects of a deviation between them (or an alteration in that spread) upon the general price level. It provides very little indication, however, on how the absolute level of either of those rates is thought to be determined. As for the natural rate, it is not defined directly but is declared to be equivalent to "the rate which would be determined by supply and demand if real capital goods were lent in kind."[19] The natural rate is sometimes described as being equal to the marginal productivity of capital on a risk-free investment project. Neither of these formulations is a usable definition for further analysis, whether theoretical or empirical, even with respect to its stated application to long-term capital loans under static conditions. Rather than definitions, they both are analogies to hypothetical loan transactions that admittedly never occur in a money economy.

Unfortunately, the concept of a "natural" level for "the" interest rate---which is questionable enough in principle---has been further beclouded in some presentations by failure to distinguish it from profit; or, more precisely, failure to specify the relationship of the supposed natural interest rate to entrepreneurial profit. One explicit statement about that relationship does say that the total product, or return, yielded on the entrepreneur's investment *minus* wages, rents, and other payments of others sets the upper limit on the interest rate (i.e., with no net return to the entrepreneur), and that the lower limit will be set by competition with other borrowers at a level "very nearly as much".[20] Stated in this way, there would seem to be little to differentiate this determination of the natural rate from that of a market rate.

The concept that at any given period there exists some unseen and unmeasured interest rate which---being shaped by fundamental, governing forces (such as the current state of the technical arts, the fecundity of capital, and a frugal abstinence)---so accurately encapsulates a country's potential for maintaining full-employment equilibrium that it could be called the natural interest rate is an idea that intrigued economists for more than a century. It joined the company of previous equally unseen but seeming verities, such as the "just price" and the Holy Grail. Ohlin decries "the domination of the curious concept of the natural rate of interest."[21]

Adherents as well as critics of neoclassical interest-rate theory felt the need for empirical confirmation. This encountered the major difficulty, candidly and voluntarily acknowledged by Wicksell: the lack of data on the natural rate for any meaningful verification. He inquires rhetorically, "how is such confirmation possible if one of the significant factors is practically an unknown? No statistics of the natural rate of interest are available." Published or survey figures on market rates could be used as surrogates only by assuming that the two rates on average are equal, he wrote, whereas "what we are looking for is the extent of the *divergence* between them, and for this there are practically no data available."[22]

Despite these obviously sincere disclaimers of hope, Wicksell nevertheless endeavored to draw some rough inferences regarding the plausibility of this theory by means of reviewing the broad three or four periods, of one or more decades each, in the preceding century during each of which the European price levels were either mainly rising or mainly falling, as the case might be. By examining whether, in each such period, the rate of industrial activity---and especially the rate of capital formation---was typically high or low, the degree of profitability, and the trend in the price level, he ventured reasoned but guarded judgements as to whether in that period the natural rate of interest was appreciably above or below the average level of the actual rates in the bond market. The principal source of price data was the set of index numbers that Jevons had calculated on the basis of the price series presented for forty groups of commodities by Tooke. In Wicksell's summary of the price-level changes in the respective periods as measured by the Tooke-Jevons series, few of the specific figures that must have provided the basis for his tentative judgments about interest movements were presented. Attention was concentrated on drawing shrewd conjectures of what "appears extremely probable" or "what must have been" the position of the natural interest rate *relative* to the market rate in order, according to his cumulative adjustment-process theory, to produce the respective price-level movements. He stated that the data did not advance his theory beyond "a mere *hypothesis*, the complete validity of which can be established only by further resort to the facts."[23]

The Market Rate in Classical Economics

In the preceding pages, we have examined only what the classical and neoclassical economists have said about the market, or money, rate of interest so far as its level relative to the "natural" rate is thought to be concerned. That relationship---in which the natural rate clearly is cast as the one of primacy---is indeed the dominant point of focus by the classical economists in regard to interest theory. Moreover, they have considered that the degree to which the respective levels of those two interest rates coincide---or move closer to, or apart from, each other---has a significant effect upon the ability of the economy to achieve or maintain the conditions of static equilibrium, which is the underlying base of neoclassical thought. But, what is said about the market rate of interest *itself*? What role is ascribed to it in the body of theory, what determines its behavior?

Answers to those questions are likely to be disappointing. Given the declaration that the level of the market interest rate will usually lie somewhere above or below that of the natural rate, sometimes for extended periods; and given that neoclassical theory emphasizes the far-reaching effects on the economy's expenditure rate and general price level that can be triggered by such a deviation between the two interest rates, one might expect that the market rate would have been accorded just as searching and systematic study as its unseen and unmeasured partner.   By and large, that has not been the case. Although there are exceptions, and although the degree and rigor of treatment vary not only across the whole group but also in different writings of the same author, the attention devoted to the actual rates in the market is generally more episodic and less analytic than that given to the abstruse "natural" rate. Just as in delineating or referring to "the" natural rate, authors also have usually spoken of "the" money, or market, rate, though with a confusing habit of sometimes alluding, in passing, to loans on real estate transactions or other non-capital credits in the same context as the bond market, without apparently noticing the inconsistency.

The author believes it possible to find at least a partial explanation, for the difference in treatment accorded to the actual, measurable rates of market interest.   That can be better done after making a brief summary of how the neoclassical economists and their predecessors dealt with the subject. For this purpose, the author draws mainly on the works of J.S. Mill and Wicksell.

One notices quite readily the perceptible difference in tone, the lower level of abstraction, and more personalized method of exposition employed by neoclassical economists when they feel called upon to deal with the market rate. Although there are many passing references to interest rates in the course of his comprehensive *Principles*, Mill gathers into one short chapter his main views of the rate of interest. From the outset, he approaches the subject in atomistic terms of the individual entrepreneur---his costs, his negotiations with the lender who supplied the borrowed funds, etc. The price-setting process is promptly labeled as obviously a matter of demand and supply in which those terms have no "different meaning or effect in this case from what they have in all others." The rate of interest emanating from that microeconomic interplay will "equalize the demand for loans with the supply of them."

Mill emphasized, however, that the two sides of the money market fluctuate "more incessantly than any other demand or supply whatsoever." Whereas pricing in other goods or services is subject to a limited number of factors, the desire to borrow and willingness to lend are influenced "by every circumstance which affects the state or prospects of industry or commerce, either generally or in any of their branches...as is shown by the never-ceasing variations in the quoted prices." Regrettably, the very small amount of tabular material, which is relegated to the *Principles'* appendix, contains no statistical data on interest rates.[24]

While classical economists indicated that interest-rate fluctuations arose from changes in either demand or supply, they observed that demand varied much more than supply. In the case of long-term capital loans, the discrepancy of demand, stronger or weaker, could persist for periods of years, e.g., during a time of war or of a boom in railroad building. Apart from cyclical factors, however, the long-term market was said to be fairly stable in volume and in interest rates. By comparison, Mill - in a rare specific reference to the short-term loan market - declared that "the *fluctuations* depend almost entirely upon the portion which is in the hands of bankers; for it is that portion almost exclusively which, being lent for short times only, is continually in the market seeking an investment." These movements in rate are held to be demand-driven, and there are even instances in which the rate on "the best mercantile bills" have varied in a year's time between four and eight or nine percent. For all borrowers of equal security, at a given time and place, the rate is uniform, and "the market rate of interest is at all times a known and definite thing."[25]

If the going rates of interest in the market were always well known to Mill, that same knowledge, if possessed later by Wicksell, was of minor interest to him. As mentioned above, in his search for any source of data that might furnish some inkling as to the (absolute) level of the elusive "natural" interest rate, he examined series on both commodity prices and market long-term rates - but only to seek whether, by comparing them with each other and with some additional figures, he might draw an inference as to where the natural rate might have been on a given date. That search proved to yield only surmises. And "if the usual direct comparison is made between the level of prices and the (market) rate of interest...a rise in prices is compatible, not only with a lower rate of interest but equally with a constant or higher rate,...for the natural rate may move further than the money rate."[26] That leaves the situation indeterminant.

If the movements of market rates could not shed any light on price-level behavior in the absence of ability to locate the natural rate, they apparently were of little use to Wicksell and his followers. To repeat, "in the last analysis, the money rate of interest depends upon the supply of and demand for *real capital*,...the rate of interest is regulated by the profits from the employment of capital itself...In addition, there is the difference between interest on short and interest on long dated loans, of which only the latter corresponds to the real rate."[27]

In sum, *short-term* lending has been largely ignored in neoclassical theory, on the ground that the rate of interest is considered a phenomenon that is fundamentally related to physical capital formation; thus the loans that possess economic significance are long-term capital loans. The "natural" interest rate on the latter is determined by the expected future net return in product, as reflected in the commodities market. Actual interest rates on loans, on the other hand, are contracted in the money market, and their price depends "in the first instance on the excess or scarcity of money."[28] Moreover, market rates of *any* maturity are judged of little consequence, since they have merely a transitional character unless and until, sooner or later, the automatic forces operating in the economy move them into coincidence with the natural rate for capital loans that is determined by the marginal productivity of capital to the borrower and the marginal utility of loanable funds to the lender. In the interval, until the actual rates prevailing in the money market move into conformity with the natural rate and equilibrium conditions are satisfied, they can be regarded as aberrations and tolerated, possibly, like mosquitos or sin.

Interest-Rate Theory in Contemporary Economics: Keynes

If one should ask what are the prevailing views of the economics profession, in the current generation, about the nature and habits of interest rates, the reply would certainly give a prominent place to the views expressed by J.M. Keynes. This is in part because of the different emphases he assigned to the forces involved in the determination of interest rates themselves, as compared with most of his predecessors of all periods; but it is also due to the large and different operational framework in which he placed the genus interest rate, along with the other macroeconomic factors. Keynes's conception of the modern capitalist economy is one endowed with essentially the same human and institutional factors as in the classical conception, but the manner in which they interact upon each other is different. The result is that the system he perceives is less self-regulating, less normative, and less likely to produce optimum results in terms of employment and output.

In order to grasp the similarities as well as the differences between the "Keynesian" school and the neoclassical tradition as they pertain to the field of our inquiry, it is appropriate to divide the search among (a) the overall systemic framework, (b) the treatment of market interest rate(s), and (c) the methods of adjustment or transition.

The Overall Framework

As the neoclassical economists saw the economy, it was either in a state of balanced equilibrium or in the fairly inexorable process of moving into that state. It seemed logical, therefore, to photograph and analyze it in that condition. Basic assumptions were that product and factor markets were perfect in the economist's technical sense (i.e., perfect as to competition, knowledge, mobility) and that full employment of human and other resources prevailed. In consequence, the levels of employment, output, and income were at or close to the maximum of which the economic system was capable, given the state of the technological arts existing at the moment. The size of the money stock would be adequate to provide the medium of exchange necessary for the prevailing volume of transactions in goods and services. The market rate of interest for (long-term capital) loans would, under the equilibrium conditions just described, be the same as the "natural rate, which was thought to correspond at all times to the expected marginal rate of return on new formation of capital given the state of the arts at that time. A dominant characteristic of this state of equilibrium was that it would maintain stability of the general price level. This price-level characteristic was considered both a logical result of the system as modeled and a major objective of economic policy.

In Keynesian economics, the notion of equilibrium is useful in understanding conditions in the economy, but there is no unique solution as to its meaning and level. This stems largely from the fact that Keynes did not accept the assumptions of full employment and of perfectly competitive conditions for products or for labor and other factors of production. His object for analysis was not an idealized economy operating at optimum rates of activity and output, but a model simulating more closely conditions in the real world. Consequently, in his major works he was less concerned with price stability than the classicists, and more concerned with actual levels of employment and production and how they were generated. The major financial instrument in the money and capital markets (and hence the relevant one for economic analysis) was, in his view, the long-term bond; and "the" interest rate was therefore the bond rate. Keynes did not reject the term "natural" interest rate completely; but he pointed out that in the real world of varying activity levels there is conceptually a different natural rate of interest (in the same neoclassical sense) for every different level of employment. "If there is" a natural rate "which is unique and significant, it must be the rate which we might term the *neutral* rate of interest, namely, the natural rate in the above sense which is consistent with *full* employment, given the other parameters of the system."[29]

Market Rates of Interest

In the immediately preceding section we saw that neoclassical economics regarded the interest rates occurring in the money markets as transitory prices arrived at by expediency or passing circumstances, and not readily incorporated into a body of theory that was primarily predicated on a state of equilibrium. What attention was given to the rate of interest was either devoted toward excogitating a theory in terms of a hypothetical "natural", physical-capital related rate or took the form of current-history comments on selected market behavior. The rate determined by the market was seen as governed by a fairly stable flow of new loanable funds, on one hand, and a more variable current demand for new capital formation on the other.

To Keynes, the market interest rate was not a matter of incidental or negligible importance: it was the rate for primary attention and analysis, and his views about its role and method of determination differed distinctly from the classical tradition. The Keynesian explanation of how interest rates are determined develops out of its views about the forces composing the economy's demand for money. Three different forces or "motives" are described in the *General Theory*. The first is the transactions motive, reflecting the need of firms and individuals to possess cash (which term is used interchangeably with money) in order to engage in transactions involving payments and other transfers. The second source of demand for money is the precautionary motive, reflecting the desire to obtain the means for meeting unexpected expenses, take advantage of unanticipated opportunities for profit, etc.

The remaining motive entering into the economy's total demand for money (i.e., for currency and transferable bank deposits) in the Keynesian listing is the speculative motive. This is the component of total money demand that is the most changeable and hence has the greatest economic influence. Persons and firms holding given sums for speculative reasons are preferring to hold liquid cash at a given time, rather than income-earning financial assets. Keynes, delineating his "liquidity-preference theory" of interest, presents it in terms of a two-asset model---bonds and cash balances---partly for expository simplicity but largely from his personal preoccupation with "the much more important long-term rates of interest."[30]   It is the liquidity-preference schedule, measuring the various amounts of money balances that the public wishes to hold at a given time, on one hand, and the present (or sometimes "available") money supply, on the other hand, that together determine the rate of interest. Keynes emphatically rejected the proposition of some economists, contemporary or past, who asserted that the interest rate is determined by the respective schedules of saving and investment, pointing out that net shifts in preference between cash and other assets reflect the diverse views of *all* holders of physical and financial assets - not merely of those persons involved in current, new-investment decisions, which was the view of the neoclassical economics.

The concept of liquidity preference and its role in determining market interest rates are presented at many passages in the *General Theory* and in subsequent writings defending this interest theory, often with slightly different formulations or emphases.   In view of the contrast with the preceding classical tradition, a sampling of two such passages provides the flavor of Keynes's never-dull prose.

1. Thus the rate of interest at any time, being the reward for parting with liquidity, is a measure of the unwillingness of those who possess money to part with their liquid control over it...It is the 'price' which equilibrates the desire to hold wealth in the form of cash with the available quantity of cash...There is, however, a necessary condition failing which...a liquidity-preference for money as a means of holding wealth could not exist. This necessary condition is the existence of uncertainty as to the future of the rate of interest.

2. The resulting theory...is...that the rate of interest on a loan of given quality and maturity has to be established at the level which, in the opinion of those who have the opportunity of choice--i.e., of wealth-holders--equalises the attractions of holding idle cash and of holding the loan...The function of the rate of interest is to modify the money-prices of other capital assets in such a way as to equalise the attraction of holding them and of holding cash.[31]

It is noteworthy, in those passages and other similar statements outlining his description of how interest rates are arrived at, that Keynes regarded the *lenders* (including potential lenders) as being the side of the market that has the major influence, indeed almost predominate influence, in determining the volume and price in the loan market. This is in contrast to the appraisal of relative market forces of neoclassical economists---when they addressed more than perfunctory attention to market rates at all---as exemplified by the observations of Mill, earlier quoted, to the effect that this market is demand-driven. Some of Keynes's colleagues have challenged this lack of balance between the respective supply and demand forces as named by him, and have objected to the concentration on the speculative portion alone, among the possible components of the demand curve for cash.[32]

A second comment about Keynes's exposition of his theory of loan price determination pertains to the relative lack of references to the determining forces in terms of *schedules*. (This is not the case with his presentation of other major determinants in his macroeconomic universe, such as the marginal efficiency of capital.) When it comes to interest rates, he tends to employ terms, like quantity or level, that connote points rather than the curves or schedules of marginalist price theory. This could merely have been for brevity, or from a belief that the reader would mentally supply the schedule image. But the sentence in the first passage above, which identifies the aggregate supply side of the market simply as "the *available quantity* of cash" (italics not in original) without relation or dependence to anything seemed elliptical to others and was noted by Ohlin in a rejoinder to Keynes.[33]

Method of Interest-Rate Transition

The Keynesian view of any relationship between market rates of interest and what neoclassical economics traditionally called a "natural" rate of interest is both clear and agnostic. As examined earlier in this chapter, the neoclassical theory is that the natural rate corresponds to the marginal product that could be expected from new investment in physical capital, and as such it exerts more or less pull upon rates contracted in the financial marketplace. When the two rates are equivalent, under the overall assumptions of full employment and perfect markets, equilibrium of the price level would be maintained. Keynes rejected these ideas, stating that there is no *unique* optimum or normative rate; and in his system of thought the only meaningful hypothetical rate in that sense would be a "neutral" rate of interest: one that is "consistent with *full* employment, given the other parameters of the system." He recognized that there is no guarantee that the forces governing the interest rate and the other parameters referred to would necessarily harmonize to produce stability in the system at the level of full employment. Thus he doubted the automaticity of the cumulative adjustment process which Wicksell and other earlier economists envisioned.[34]

Other Contemporary Theories on Interest

So far in this section on interest theory in contemporary economics, attention has been focussed on the views propounded by Keynes on the role of interest rates in the economic system and the manner in which the long-term rate is set. While there are cogent reasons, as expressed at the outset, for devoting this sort of attention to the position of that writer and his followers, mention should also be made of certain other theories that have developed and that enjoy varying degrees of support. One obvious such theory, of course, is the basic neoclassical analysis which we have already examined at some length and which, with occasional minor refinements, still maintains many adherents, particularly in some European countries. To recapitulate briefly, the writers of that group describe the natural interest rate on new long-term capital loans as being determined by demand and supply forces representing, respectively, the entrepreneurs' expected marginal rate of return on prospective new investment, and the lenders' supply curve of loanable funds.[35]

It has been apparent in our comparison of neoclassical and Keynesian views about interest that both of them envision the determination of "the" rate as involving a negotiation or resolution of highly-aggregated views of buyers and of sellers---a method of price resolution that in the end is invariably and unavoidably expressed in the generality of "by the forces of demand and supply." On the whole, what divides one theory of interest from the others is the manner in which it perceives or identifies what the elements are, at the next-lower level of abstraction, that *compose* the demand or supply forces. In short, the demand for what, the supply of what?

Like the sixteenth century Reformation in the field of religion, the twentieth century developments in economic and monetary theory started out more as a re-ordering and remodeling than as an insurrection, though Keynes's *General Theory* provoked a number of scholarly and popular references by others to the "Keynesian revolution." Again, like the Reformation, there is not just one but a number of Luthers and Zwinglis whose writings before and after World War II intensified and advanced the development of monetary economics. While much attention of monetary theorists has been devoted to other branches of this broad subject such as the fluctuations in economic activity, price-level changes, inflation, and the balance of international payments, the subject of interest has not been ignored. Only a few additional theories of the interest rate need be mentioned here, both because of limited space and because some are duplicative.

Writers who share Keynes's emphasis on the importance of the levels of national income and employment, as forces for macroeconomic analysis, nevertheless are convinced that the liquidity preference theory of interest should be supplemented, if not supplanted, by a formulation broad enough to include other components. Lutz acknowledges that if money wage rates are assumed to be rigid, the quantity of money and the liquidity preference schedule do influence "indeed not only employment and national income but also the rate of interest. But even here...the marginal efficiency of investment and the rate of saving are determinants of the rate of interest alongside the monetary factor."[36]

Some of the most articulate and sometimes sharply-worded discussions of comparative views about the determination of interest rates took place in professional journals in the several years after the publication of Keynes's major book.[37] Participants in this lively discussion were mainly British and American economists and a few others who were themselves contributing to the development of monetary theory and policy and macroeconomics in general. One anomaly apparent in the exchange first-listed is that whereas Keynes was absolute in his conviction that his view of interest-rate determination was "radically" different from those of his contemporaries, these latter were equally convinced that they were all in agreement in substance, if not in terminology.[38] It is clear that Keynes and all three writers of rejoinders to him rejected any formulation that asserted that the rate of interest is determined by the demand and supply of savings, or that it equalizes the volume of saving and investment. Where the three differ from Keynes is in the explanation that these three (in large concurrence with each other) presented to *replace* the rejected statement. The essence of this replacement lies in the concept of *credit* (=claims).

To expand slightly on Ohlin's thesis,[39] a market rate of interest is the price of credit, meaning that it is fixed in the money market where the rate or rates are determined by the demand and supply curves for various types of old and new financial claims to assets, and where the quantities of both cash and other assets influence the pricing process. The author accepts this view, but only to the extent that it is a more comprehensive statement about the long-term bond rate than those of either Keynes or other principal schools of thought. Like these others, however, it is addressed only to the bond market; moreover, like most other interest theories, it is pitched at such a high level of abstraction that attempts at empirical verification are extremely difficult. Demand and supply curves for financial claims are not known or published in advance. And even *ex post* they do not leave behind them paths or footprints, but only the point of their fleeting tryst, the point where they intersected to conceive the rate of interest.

Given the focus of this book on a particular, and particularly significant, type of credit, the author has been especially eager to distinguish what positions have been taken by theoretical economists about *short-term* loans to the non-financial business sector. This would be prudent even as a precautionary step, as routine scientific procedure, rather than to assume that what has been written about long-term bonds and their interest rates would equally apply to short-term lending. The fact that writers on interest theory from the early 1800s to the present day have explicitly and consistently asserted that "the" interest rate they were addressing is the long-term capital rate also implies a second but related assertion: that they regard the long- and short-term markets as separate and different.[40] The further judgement they make, without corroboration, that long-term loans are the only ones of macroeconomic significance should not deter us. Evidence on the magnitude and the functions performed by short-term loans was presented in Chapters 2 and 3.

In light of our objective stated above, it can be disappointing to author and reader alike to confirm that, on the whole, the professional literature has said very little that is germane, meaningful, or incisive about the short-term loan operations that occur continuously between banks and business firms, and the interest rates attaching thereto; and some things that have been written are superficial. The preceding sentence applies to the majority of writers of whatever period or school - to those whose theoretical output constituted what was currently considered the mainstream of economic thought in a given period. Fortunately, there is a handful of economists who *have* given substantive attention to the short-term loan market in one or more aspects, and we shall summarize their contributions below.

It is significant that the tendency on the part of several economists to depart from the common practice of denigrating, if not ignoring, the role of short-term credit in the economic system is almost exclusively a mid-20th century development. This stems not so much from changes in the economy itself---though structural and operational alterations in the economy and the monetary system have, of course, occurred---as it stems from changes in the approach adopted by some economists for analyzing economic processes. Specifically, this reflects a shift from constructing and studying a model of a closed economy in a state of stationary equilibrium, under conditions of perfect factor and product markets and full employment of resources, to a model that as far as possible avoids abstracting from the advances, economic mutations, and even exogenous shocks that in reality occur in an evolving economy, and that takes account of the institutional framework within which the banking system and the monetary authority operate. Moreover, the relevant contributions come largely from certain economists concerned in some manner with the objectives and tools of macroeconomic policy conducted by the central banks of industrialized countries.

Contributions regarding the economic and monetary role of short-term business loans have effectively elucidated the manner in which working capital borrowed from banks finances activity in the commodity markets; how it affects and is affected by movements in the level of aggregate demand and income; how individual banks can, and sometimes do, exercise a degree of judgement over the volume and interest rate on loans to a particular borrower or sector; and the manner in which lenders and borrowers in the short-term market react to monetary-control actions (and signals) emanating from the central bank. While the writings referred to usually refrain from formulating a unique or stylized theory of "how the rate of interest is determined" in the fashion of Keynes or the neoclassical economists speaking of the long-term rate, there are indications from which one can infer their views about the pricing of loans at commercial banks. Among the authors who have, at some time, devoted serious analytic attention to the short-term market for bank loans to commercial and industrial borrowers are Hawtrey, Roosa, Lutz, and Robertson, and the present precis draws on their relevant works.

To those authors, it was important to emphasize that the greater part of the short-term borrowing is for the purpose of providing working capital to business firms operating in all sectors of the commodity markets (see Chapter 2 above). This fact had not been absorbed--if perceived--by previous writers. Even to some of the late 19th and 20th century economists who have written on capital and interest, the short-term loan is considered primarily as a substitute for a long-term securitized loan at times when the availability or interest rate on the latter became unfavorable; and the subject is sometimes treated in the context of the term structure on *capital* loans.[41] Even Marshall had seemed to believe that only "speculators" would acquire commodities with borrowed money. In contrast, Hawtrey carefully traced the various patterns by which merchants and manufacturers acquire or hold stocks of materials as well as finished goods, financed by short-term bank credits, during normal business conditions. Banks, even in prosperous times, sometimes vary their terms or lending volume to a given customer or sector. At times of turning points in the cycle, according to the authors under review, the banks were found to be more sensitive to changes in interest rates than the borrowers, partly because of the implications for their existing loan portfolios.[42]

Among questions which absorbed attention from these authors was the comparison between the short- and long-term rates of interest, both of which they obviously regarded as tangible, ascertainable market rates rather than as conceptualized "natural" or normative loan prices. Empirical data were quoted to show that long rates differed from short rates in the amplitude of their fluctuations, with the long-term figures typically showing much smaller and less frequent movements. In addition to these differences in pattern, they found that variations in long-term rates were relatively little influenced by rates in the short market.

These findings not only helped to establish the facts that both markets are important but are separate in behavior; they also related directly to the debate that was carried on sporadically in the period from 1930 to the 1950s over the efficacy of central banks' monetary control, particularly in the United Kingdom and the United States. Neoclassical economics (and even Keynes), proceeding from their traditional identification of interest with the subject of capital formation, had taken the position that monetary policy depended for its success on being able to influence the long end of the interest spectrum;[43] and they attributed any shortcomings in the Bank of England's efforts or those of the Federal Reserve to their inability to control the bond rate. Since they tended to attribute that failure to the existence, in both countries, of a huge war-time accumulation of governmental debt securities, the task of monetary control appeared doomed to some writers. In rebuttal to those conclusions, the contributions from Roosa and Hawtrey marshalled data on the size of the working-capital market, its sensitivity to interest-rate changes, and the possibility of turning the stock of government securities into a useful tool, rather than obstruction, to central bank control measures.

They pointed out that a change of the central bank's discount rate had been designed from the beginning to impinge promptly on working capital, and while commercial banks have diminished their resort to the discount window, especially in the U.S., the volume of government securities provided ample ammunition for conducting the central bank's open-market operations, which had become a potent and more frequently-used tool than the discount window anyhow. Despite its "decisive power over the short-term rate of interest", the monetary authority can produce only limited effects upon the long rates, in Hawtrey's view.[44]

The temporary disillusionment with the monetary-control record of the central banks that was then current, Roosa pointed out, came partly from the misconception that the impact of interest-rate manipulation would be solely on borrowers and savers. He demonstrated the effects on bank lenders, and their behavioral responses, in the light of institutional changes in the financial market and in central bank techniques. Rate changes affect to some extent the decisions of all economic agents who save, borrow, or lend, including corporate decisions on dividend distribution *vs.* reinvestment, but the impact on lenders is usually greater.[45]

A curious fact, alluded to two-three pages above, is that those writers who devoted the most thorough and perspicacious examination of short-term lending to business firms have not offered an explicit theory of how short-term interest rates are "determined".[46] As summarized here, they have explored the importance of this credit instrument in financing the working capital required throughout the commodity markets, the relation of that body of working capital to the productive process and its behavior in different cyclical phases of the economy, and the influence exerted by the monetary-control measures of the Federal Reserve upon the existing portfolio of such loans and new additions to it. These few authors, however, have abstained from presenting a summary formula on the determination of short-term rates analogous to those formulae propounded by others for long-term capital loans. As we have observed in this chapter, the latter theories have typically taken the form of stating that "the" rate of interest is determined by the forces of demand and supply that are aggregated conceptually in two schedules or curves on a two-dimensional diagram relating volumes of money to rates of interest per annum---a downward-sloping demand curve and an upward-sloping supply curve. These theories attempt to diagnose and label the human motives or objectives that account, in the proponent's view, for the shape and slope of these curves by such summary terms as abstinence, time preference, impatience, productivity, liquidity preference, investment opportunity. The current rate of interest is identified with and determined by the point at which the hypothesized two curves, as constituted at a given moment, intersect.

Although the writings of Hawtrey and Roosa cited above asserted no comparable generalized formulation for determination of short-term rates in the banking market, it seems possible to attribute to them, by inference, the outlines of the position they hold. As a starting point, they share the knowledge of many others that short-term rates fluctuate more than long rates, and that rates react to various market developments and to expected ones. They add their finding that participants in this market are sensitive to changes which affect the cost and availability of funds to themselves, and that this applies to changes originating in the money market, in the commodity markets, or in the actions of the central bank. They pay particular attention to the vigilance of the modern central bank and also to its willingness to employ the control instruments at its disposal on a continuing basis to produce movements in the volume and interest cost of the reserve holding of the commercial banking system. "In quiet conditions credit responds easily to moderate upward and downward movements" of interest rates engineered by the monetary authority; and if the central bank's actions were always "*initiated in time,* the conditions need never be other than quiet in a monetary sense." Roosa, perhaps even more cognizant of the changeability of market conditions and of the differing responses to a given change in direction, stresses the "continuous close study" carried on by the Federal Reserve of the underlying and transitory developments, as well as the agility with which it acts either to increase a certain pressure or to reverse it.[47]

To synthesize the preceding paragraph, the Federal Reserve closely monitors to judge the appropriate development of reserves in the banking system, and at its discretion takes action to augment or reduce that volume, which usually alters the rate of federal funds from what it might otherwise have been in the absence of that action. To shape a short summary in the curved language and aphoristic style of interest-rate theories, the federal funds rate is determined at the intersection of the curves embodying the forces of demand and supply in the market for interbank loan funds.[48] Actions taken by the Fed to inject or extract money from the banking system's reserves certainly produce both a tangible change in those resources and a signal-giving effect. It is a debatable proposition, however, whether one can proceed to declare that the interbank loan rate is wholly "determined" by the central bank; and it is even more conjectural whether Hawtrey and

Roosa were tacitly saying that. Perhaps the most that should be concluded is that it is more productive to illuminate the ways in which - within the evolving economic and technical framework - the tools of monetary policy can be deployed to help in *maintaining* (or producing a desired *change* in) a given level of short-terms interest rates and credit availability, rather than to compose a satisfactory aphorism of static nature about original rate determination in the abstract.

Before closing this résumé of what those writers on interest theory who have gone beyond the consideration of bonds and other securitized capital loans to give some attention to the short-term market have contributed with regard to lending by commercial banks, mention should be made of passages written by two additional authors, despite the brevity or other shortcomings of their comments. One of these is Lutz. In the second edition of his *The Theory of Interest*, he inserted one chapter referring to the banking system. This is limited to modeling how commercial banks would achieve optimum composition (i.e., profit maximization) of their assets, provided that their choices were confined to bonds, Treasury bills, or overnight loans to the federal funds market. The model excludes a bank's own loans to others from this exercise at the outset, declaring that "the rate on bank loans...is not a free market rate." This presumably refers to the absence of a public secondary market and published quotations for bank loans to business and others. While the Lutz exercise thus does not address the determination of bank lending rates, it is cited here for its negative implications and, in part, for comparison with a brief remark of Bertil Ohlin.[49]

In the course of a rejoinder to Keynes, Ohlin states that the price of bonds, the long-term interest rate, "is fixed on the bond market by the demand and supply curves" in the same auction-like way as eggs in a village market or wheat in the commodity exchanges. In a footnote he adds that a more complete analysis would need to consider that "only certain interest rates like the bond yield are determined in a fashion similar to commodities...Only for them is the supply and demand curve analysis practical. Other interest rates, like the discount rates, are fixed by the lenders---the central and commercial banks."[50] One might remonstrate that conceptualized supply and demand curves might be no less realistic in the banking field than in the commodity exchanges. But it is more important to observe that, both here and in the Lutz reference, there is the seed of a proposition, which can be verbalized tentatively as follows: that the short-term bank loan and its market characteristics are indeed different from the conventionally studied securities-market loans; that the importance of the role of bank credit in the system warrants further professional analysis; that the modality and basis of short-term loan pricing might, in the process, be found to be capable of explanation by different, or additional, forces than those traditionally identified in interest theory.   This possibility should be examined further, and that can best be done in the context of Chapter 7.

In the course of the last few pages, we observed how certain contemporary economists have focused not upon how lending rates in the short-term loan market are originally "determined" in some sense by the interaction of two competing schedules of demand and supply, but rather on how an existing rate level is *moved* upward or downward, either by developments in the commodity and money markets themselves or by policy actions taken by the central bank. That discussion is an important example of the shift of analytic attention, from searching for the conditions that satisfy a hypothesized equilibrium situation at a point in time, to an intertemporal focus on the means of adaptation toward the monetary stance that seems appropriate for the system in the next-after-today's economic situation.

Other examples exist in the theory of interest that involve actual or presumptive intertemporal relationships, either between the levels of the interest rate on a given financial instrument on two separate dates or the relation between the current rate on a given instrument and the general price level at some different date.   An element that is commonly shared among these various cases is the inclusion of some assumption about the kind of expectations held by market participants about the future date.   Reference has already been made earlier, for instance, to Wicksell's reiterated view that businessmen generally hold the expectation that present prices in the commodity markets will remain constant---a supposition which was rejected by Ohlin.[51]

Perhaps the best-known example of a possible intertemporal linkage believed to affect market interest rates concerns the putative impact of an anticipated inflation (otherwise expressed, of an increase in the expected rate of inflation).   Harrod declared that "A large array of economists of the highest standing have in the past propounded the view that the prospect of inflation tends to raise the rate of interest. And this view is still widely held by distinguished economists."[52] Keynes, though indubitably distinguished, was not one of those who accepted the described relationship.   The most convinced and thorough propounder of that thesis was Fisher, whose conclusions can be stated briefly as follows.   If a rise occurs in the generally-expected rate of increase in the general price level for the near future of 1 percentage point (say, from zero to a rate of 1 percent), this will cause the expected rate of return on physical capital assets to rise also by 1 percentage point, as well as an equal increase of 1 point in the yield on bonds and bills. While the Fisher theory acknowledges that, if the jump in price expectations is sudden, there will be momentary benefits to debtors and pains to lenders, but the adjustment will be rapid. New prices and yields on assets will promptly emerge, leaving relative positions unaffected, and the economy's path will be maintained with about the same level of employment and real income.

Although the fact has been commonly observed that current movements of prices and of interest rates usually are in the same general direction, the respective changes differ in timing and degree between those two groups and also as among the many individual items within the groups. These differentials across commodities and services and across asset yields are in marked contrast to the Fisherian image of an orderly and highly uniform indexation *backward* onto the current economy from a future development that is supposedly correctly as well as uniformly foreseen by economic agents. Attribution of an assumed perfect or near-perfect foresight to the holders of this theory would probably be acknowledged. For Fisher, it was not only an assumption but a virtual belief. "It is important to emphasize the broad fact that, in general, business foresight exists and that the accuracy and power of this foresight is greater today than ever before...Multitudes of trade journals" supply data on which to base prediction. "Is it reasonable to believe that foresight...has an exception as applied to falling or rising prices?"[53]

Additional assumptions embodied in this thesis are that all asset yields are determined in auction markets, transaction costs are zero, and that the changed expectation about the rate of general inflation does not involve changes in relative prices. If the assumed conditions are not fulfilled, a changed expectation about future inflation will not be neutral and uniform in its effect on today's asset holdings and today's commodity and money markets. Okun has demonstrated meticulously the actual operational and institutional characteristics of the U.S. and other industrialized economies that do not conform to the assumed responses and characteristics embodied, expressly or implicitly, in the Fisher theory and that thus seriously compromise its validity.[54]

Summary: The Present State of Short-term Interest Theory

The economics profession arrived at the closing decades of the twentieth century with a fair degree of consensus among its members about the theory of interest---more exactly, about those parts of the territory they had chosen to explore. Interest theory has been marked by two dominant characteristics: First, being preoccupied with the exploding growth over the past 170 years of physical capital (that youngest of the "three factors of production"), writers devoted theoretical attention almost solely to long-term loans--bonds--as being the chief capital-related financial instrument. Second, with varying degrees of rigor, economic theorists have conducted the study of interest within the framework of an economy assumed to be in a state of equilibrium under conditions of full employment, perfect competition and mobility, and auction-like markets for all transactions. What emerges from models so framed is mainly the concept of *the* "natural" rate of long-term interest, which would be governed by the net rate of return expected on new investment at the given state of the technical arts. This natural rate is freely acknowledged to be a hypothetical, normative concept, neither measured, measurable, nor fixed over time.

Existence of actual, quoted interest rates on long-term loan instruments was known, of course, to economic theorists, who referred to the rates in the singular (as with the natural rate) as "the" market or money rate. But much less systematic analysis was given to the market rates, long- or short-term, even though, unlike the amorphous "natural" rate, they are transactional prices actually employed between agents in the economic process.

In rare cases, however, the spotlight was briefly focused on true lending rates in the market. The main elements of received doctrine about market lending rates, long and short, include the following:

* Mill flatly called the pricing process on long-term loans a microeconomic interplay of demand and supply no different in meaning from "all others", ostensibly labeling it as a case for partial-equilibrium treatment like any given commodity. This viewpoint is widely shared by others.
* He went on to observe, though, that the "never-ceasing variations" in bond quotations indicate that, in contrast with markets for other products, the participants in the loan market are influenced by every circumstance affecting the outlook for the economy, in general or in any sector.While this observation plainly was a recognition that, on the demand side, participants in the loan market come from a broad variety of sectors, it is doubtful whether it also implied that pricing in the bond market must only be treated within a

general-equilibrium model.

* The forces that compose the demand and supply curves in the loan market of assumed auction pricing have been described in diverse ways. One formulation states that the price determined by the curves depends in the short run on the excess or scarcity of loanable money, and in the long run on the net return from the employment of physical capital. The Keynesian view is that the bond rate, in the short run, is determined by the relative preference at a given moment between holding liquid cash rather than earning assets, on one hand, and the quantity of loanable funds, on the other hand. A third example, from the Stockholm theory, is that the bond rate is determined by the demand and supply curves for credit, the make-up of which at any given time embodies the combined effects of several different factors, including the disposition of persons and institutions to save and invest, which is itself affected by the current rate of interest, the national income, the monetary policy of the central bank, and "the whole economic process."

* A theory as complex as the one last cited, with many major ingredients of both static and dynamic nature, can not easily be handled as a standard case of price determination in an individual industry market.

* Difficulties encountered when one lifts the veil of abstraction to see what multiple factors are bundled into the two schedules of demand and supply may have led some authors to readjust the analytic focus away from interest-rate "determination" and toward the subject of rate movements or changes, as indicated by the following declared findings.

* In the market for securities, the interest rates on shorter-term instruments can, in principle, be expected to be lower than on the longer-term ones.

* Short-term rates fluctuate more frequently than long-term rates.

* Among time series of short- and long-term rates, changes of slope of the two curves are usually in the same direction.

* An upward movement of interest rates is frequently experienced in periods when the general price level is rising, and a downward movement in periods of falling prices.

* Changes in short-term rates often occur in response to monetary-control actions taken by the central bank, to whose actions they are sensitive.

* Changes in short-term rates can also result from shifts in the public's total demand for financial assets or in its preferences among those assets.

* Rare and scarcely-noticed suggestions have been made that, in the case of short-term bank loans, the lending rates do not, in practice, result from an auction or equivalent procedure but are set in a different, less-negotiated fashion.

Notes

1. In medieval usage, the term *usury* meant the lending of money under terms requiring a return to the lender greater than the principal amount of the loan; i.e., making an interest-bearing loan. In modern usage, usury has gradually come to mean the charging of an interest rate judged, by a statutory or other defined standard, as excessive or rapacious. See Roll 1974, pp. 47-50; Spiegel 1983, pp. 63-65.

2. See Spiegel 1987, p. 769.

3. Roll, pp. 51-59. Moreover, in the 14-15th centuries some lenders in Florence and Venice were engaged in both foreign-exchange operations and deposit banking. Interest hurdles in the latter branch could sometimes be surmounted by imaginative exchange transactions masking a loan-interest component. *Cf.* Spiegel 1983, pp. 67-69.

4. See Patinkin 1968, p. 473; Usher 1943, pp. 170-175.

5. The components of M1, as currently defined, are (a) currency in circulation; (b) travelers checks outstanding; (c) demand deposits at commercial banks, other than certain excluded holdings; and (d) other checkable deposits at depository institutions. Each component is more precisely defined in notes to the table on money stock in the monthly *Federal Reserve Bulletin*.

6. The Latin phrase refers to a lender's lost or missed opportunity for economic gain by virtue of diverting funds from some other alternative enterprise.

7. Buchanan 1987, p. 718, and Buchanan 1969, Chapter 2; Robbins 1970, p. 18.

8. *E.g.*, the choice of a person or firm to hold cash (currency or demand deposits) can be influenced by the rate available on a time deposit, Treasury bill, etc. See Brown 1987, pp. 51-54.

9. In presenting the views of the classical school, the author draws mainly on the works of Ricardo, Smith, Thornton, and J.S. Mill.

10. Ricardo 1821, Chapter XXI, esp. pp. 280-284; Mill 1848, pp. 405-407..

11. Cf. Panico 1987, pp. 877-879.

12. Thornton 1802, pp. 252-256; Mill, pp. 638 and 642-647; Ricardo 1811, p. 35.

13. Keynes 1937, pp. 250-252.

14. See, for example, Wicksell 1898, *Interest and Prices*, pp. 108-109, pp. 120-121; Wicksell 1906, *Lectures on Political Economy*, Vol. 2, pp. 194-200.

15. *Interest and Prices*, p. xxvi.

16. Ibid., pp. 106-110: and *Lectures*, pp. 190-191.

17. *Lectures*, pp. 193-208.

18. In his introduction to the English translation of Wicksell's *Lectures*, Robbins said, "For more advanced students...and for readers of maturity it is admirably fitted...I know of no single work better suited to the needs of any natural scientist who wishes to get a general view of what theoretical economics is about." Robbins 1934, in Wicksell 1906, *Lectures*, p. xxi.

19. Wicksell, *Interest and Prices*, pp. 102-104.

20. *Interest and Prices*, pp. 102-104.

21. Ohlin in *Interest and Prices*, Introduction, p. xii.

22. *Interest and Prices*, Chapter 11.

23. Ibid, p. 176.

24. Quoted passages in this and the preceding paragraph are from Mill 1848, *Principles*, p. 637 and p. 638.

25. Ibid., p. 640 and p. 411, respectively.

26. Wicksell 1898, p. 107. The word "market" is absent, but implied, in the original. In addition to the difference between Mill and Wicksell in their degree of attention to current market rates, they held somewhat different views about market expectations regarding the price level. In contrast to Mill's description of market sensitivity to the "smallest circumstance" and "smallest breath of probable gain" (*Principles*, pp. 411 and 638), Wicksell in several passages declared that businessmen do not count on future changes in prices "but, on the contrary, normally proceed on the assumption that present prices of commodities will remain constant." See, e.g., *Lectures*, Vol. 2, p. 185.

27. Wicksell, *Lectures*, Vol. 2, pp. 190-191.

28. Wicksell, *Interest and Prices*, p. 108.

29. Keynes 1936, p. 243.

30. Ibid., p. 197.

31. Keynes 1936, pp. 167-168; and Keynes 1937, p. 250.

32. Robertson 1937, pp. 433-434.

33. Ohlin 1937, p. 423, p. 425.

34. See Keynes 1936, pp. 242-244, and Harrod's comments thereon, in Harrod 1969, p. 175 and pp. 177-178.

35. Irving Fisher, though his work on capital theory and interest was grounded in the work of Boehm-Bawerk and other neoclassical economists, wrote about a growing, rather than stationary, economy. His theory was confined completely, however, to the capital market. His brief passage referring to short-term loans was perhaps an after-thought, descriptive and at an elementary level. Fisher, 1930, pp. 359-363.

36. Lutz 1968, p. 208.

37. E.g., see Keynes's reply to various reviews of his *General Theory* in *The Economic Journal*, June 1937, and the three rejoinders of Ohlin, Robertson, and Hawtrey in that *Journal*, September 1937 (in this book, listed by name of author and the year 1937).

38. Keynes 1937, pp. 241-245. Lutz emphatically dismisses the debate about the equivalence of the liquidity-preference and the loanable-funds theory as an "intensive discussion on a problem of formal logic...which does not really deserve the efforts devoted to it." Lutz, p. 208.

39. See Ohlin 1937, pp. 426-427.

40. A variant view sometimes encountered is that firms which borrow on short terms are doing so *mainly* as second choice---as a substitute for a long-term capital loan they would normally prefer. See, e.g., Robertson 1959, p. 77. While instances of this type occur, the majority of C + I loans are at short term because these maturities fit the borrowers' working-capital plans and needs.

41. For the latter point, see Lutz, pp. 252-276.

42. Hawtrey 1937a, pp. 82-85, 111-119, 193-199. The views of Marshall cited above come from his evidence before the Gold and Silver Commission in 1888, briefly referred to in Hawtrey 1937a, his p. 112. On banks' discretionary responses, see Hodgman 1963, pp. 29-31.

43. Keynes indeed held similar views: that the rate on bonds was the relevant rate to be influenced by central bank action, and that the volume of investment in working capital is not sensitive to changes in short-term interest rates. See his *General Theory*, p. 197, and the commentaries thereon by Hawtrey 1937a, p. 116, and Harrod 1969, p. 179.

44. Hawtrey, op. cit., p. 193.

45. Roosa 1951, pp. 275-277, 286-287. Robertson 1953-1954, pp. 138-141, partly influenced by the restraints on the effectiveness of Bank of England measures produced by the exceptions and distortions practiced in the 1950s by U.K. capital-market policies, was more skeptical than Roosa of the sensitivity of the short-term market.

46. I believe that Fisher's position with regard to actual market rates of interest was very similar in substance to that of Hawtrey and Roosa, and more explicitly stated than theirs. This resemblance has not always been grasped. Fisher was dedicated primarily to developing a theory of interest, but simultaneously he was intrigued and frustrated by the complications in the real world that confront attempts at confirmation. "This book is intended to be study in pure theory. As such, its ultimate objective is to explain how the rate of interest would be determined *in vacuo* or under the ideal operation of the assumptions." Within that sheltered vacuum, he asserted the possibility of marshalling all operative factors into two aggregated forces, the Impatience to spend income and the profitable Opportunity to invest it. But once "outside this domain, there are literally thousands of forces" to be analyzed "before an adequate explanation of an actual market rate of interest could be made." He identified in broad terms some of those forces. But again, "It is impossible to

present a verification of any theory of interest...at all times the economic causes tending to make interest high are combined with others tending to make it low." Thus, like Hawtrey and Roosa, he did not formulate an explanation of how a market rate is "determined," but instead studied how those rates *move* as the result of market influences or of central bank action. For him, the focus was wholly on the bond rate, whereas for Roosa and Hawtrey the focus included short-term rates. Fisher 1930, pp. 487-488 and p. 372.

47. The quoted passages are from Hawtrey 1937a, p. 122, and from Roosa, pp. 286-287.

48. See Goodfriend and Whelpley 1986, especially pp. 11-15.

49. Lutz 1968, pp. 277-278.

50. Ohlin 1937, p. 424.

51. Ohlin 1936, p. xii.

52. Harrod 1969, pp. 179-181. In this brief and somewhat rambling passage Harrod mentions some of his own and Keynes's views about what effects the prospect of inflation might exert, e.g., on the yield of equities and real estate as compared with bonds.

53. Fisher 1896, *Appreciation and Interest*. The passages quoted are from a long paragraph wholly devoted to establishing this point; pp. 378-379 of the 1965 reprint.

54. In the course of effectively refuting the neat and neutral claims of the Fisher theory, Okun indicates the diverse kinds of distortions and other effects that are indeed produced or exacerbated by inflation and the prospect of it. Okun 1981, pp. 208-217. See also Summers 1983, pp. 201-233.

5

Empirical Evidence:
Contributing But Not Conclusive

> No matter how plausible all this may appear, it is only facts themselves that can provide final confirmation..., and practical applications should be the goal of every theory.
>
> ---Knut Wicksell, *Interest and Prices*

> It is impossible to present a verification of any theory of interest. The facts are too meager, too conflicting, and too intermixed to admit of clear analysis and precise interpretation.
>
> ---Irving Fisher, *The Theory of Interest*

The preceding chapter presented a survey of the views expressed by contemporary economists as well as their predecessors with regard to the phenomenon of interest and especially to the rates of interest. The body of received economic thought on this subject can be roughly divided into three unequal parts: (a) findings and premises concerning the behavior of interest rates over time, alone, or in relation to other economic variables; (b) hypotheses or conclusions as to the factors that determine interest rates---which is the part generally considered as the core of the theory of interest; and (c) hypotheses concerning the role that interest rates themselves play, in turn, in determining the economy's macroeconomic position.

In the present chapter, the objective is to examine empirical data that pertain to one or another component of the theoretical material we have reviewed and, to the extent possible, to judge whether there is a reasonable correspondence between the findings of theory and the ascertainable facts. In embarking on this task, one must keep in mind that in the professional literature the focus has been almost exclusively upon the capital market and the long-term bond, whereas the object of this book's inquiry is the short-term bank loan to nonfinancial business firms. In addition, much of this work on "the" long-term bond rate adopted an analytical model that posits an economy characterized by full employment of human and other resources and by perfect product and factor markets.   Clearly, most economists writing about the lending function and the types of loans and interest rates have recognized the long-term capital loan as *different* in character and operation from the short-term lending carried on by the banking system, on one hand; but also have thought it to be of much greater economic significance, on the other hand..

It is logical, therefore, that the starting-point should be to look at available data that may aid in clarifying the nature and extent of such differences or similarities. Obviously, many business firms need, at one time or another, to approach the bond market or the commercial banks for credit, the choice depending upon the nature of their financial requirements at the time.   How do the long-term bond industry and the short-term commercial banks compare, for example, in their coverage of the nonfinancial corporate sector in the United States?   Statistics are available which, although not ideally matched, permit an approximate measurement on this point for the ten-year period 1972-1982.[1]   Table 5.1 provides, for each of the six even-numbered years in that period, the percent distribution of commercial and industrial loans outstanding (by industry group of borrower) at large commercial banks. The numbered rows in the table have been slightly regrouped to facilitate comparisons with the less-detailed breakdown by industry group in Table 5.2 on corporate bond issues for identical years. This latter table presents the percent distribution of new bond issues (not bonds outstanding) for all corporations except for the category "real estate and financial", the latter being deleted so as to conform with the content of banks' C+I loans.   The author believes that juxtaposing of stock (loans outstanding) data in one table with new-issue data in the other, while usually questionable procedure, does not seriously affect comparing the respective breakdowns by industry group.

Some similarities are evident in the industrial composition of borrowers in the two credit markets. Manufacturers form a large component among both the bond issuers and the bank borrowers, for example; and transportation companies typically accounted for only 5-8 percent of all loans in both tables. Differences, however, are more numerous than similarities. Variance over time is striking in the bond issues, where manufacturing's share ranged from 23.9 percent to 43.8,

TABLE 5.1 C+I Loans Outstanding at Large Commercial Banks, by Industry Group (percent distribution, at 4 quarterly dates)

	1972	1974	1976	1978	1980	1982
TOTAL, in billion dollars	71.1	104.4	91.8	109.7	142.8	186.7
1. Manufacturing	33.1	34.8	32.0	31.4	30.0	28.4
2. Trade, distribution, and services	28.5	27.3	28.5	31.5	32.3	30.4
a. Commodity dealers	2.1	2.0	1.9	1.9	1.4	1.0
b. Other wholesalers	6.9	6.6	7.1	8.8	8.3	7.2
c. Retail	6.8	6.9	7.2	8.0	8.1	7.0
d. Services industries	12.8	11.8	12.3	12.8	14.5	15.3
3. Transportation	8.2	6.1	6.4	5.2	5.2	4.8
4. Public utilities	3.7	6.7	6.8	4.9	5.9	5.6
5. Communication	2.1	2.2	1.9	1.6	2.0	2.5
6. Mining (incl. oil and gas)	4.9	4.0	7.2	8.8	9.6	14.8
7. Construction	6.1	5.9	4.9	4.7	4.1	4.1
8. All other	13.2	13.1	12.4	11.9	10.9	9.3
TOTAL, in percent	100.0	100.0	100.0	100.0	100.0	100.0

TABLE 5.2 New Bond Issues of Corporations, by Industry Group
(percent distribution; average of four quarterly dates)

	1972	1974	1976	1978	1980	1982
Total Corporate bond issues (all industry groups except "Real Estate & financial"[a]), billions of dollars	1.509	2.487	2.138	1.825	4.731	3.054
Industry Group, percent of total						
1. Manufacturing	23.9	43.8	37.7	40.8	42.3	37.0
2. Commercial & miscellaneous	17.9	5.4	14.0	15.7	8.0	18.9
3. Transportation	4.4	6.3	11.8	7.8	5.9	5.0
4. Public utility	25.3	29.9	30.3	7.8	15.0	30.8
5. Communication	28.5	14.7	6.3	27.9	28.7	8.3
	100.0%	100.0%	100.0%	100.0%	100.0%	100.0%

a.   This group in published series is omitted here for comparability with
     C+I bank loans, which include no loans to real estate or financial companies.

Source: Federal Reserve *Annual Statistical Digest*, various years. Figures represent gross proceeds
          of issues maturing in more than one year.

whereas short-term bank loans for that group ranged only between 28 and 34.8 percent of the total. The communication industry, which issued about 28 percent of all bonds in half of the years covered, registered only 6 percent in 1976. Lending to public utility corporations by commercial banks did not exceed the 4-7 percent level, in contrast to the bond market, where utilities normally were the second-largest group. But utility bonds dropped from 30 to 7.8 percent from 1976 to 1978. In total dollar volume of all loans issued, the bond series also exhibits more year-to-year swings than the issuance of C+I loans, although on this point the portfolio data in Table 5.1 are a much less reliable basis for comparing the two markets than will be presented later.

The tables also demonstrate the greater breadth, across industries, of bank lending to nonfinancial firms than of bond financing. One example is, as expected, in the fairly large share of bank loans taken by firms engaged in trade and distribution.[2] Working capital requirements in all branches of industry are largely financed by C+I loans, as we have noted in Chapter 4 and elsewhere, but the inventory components of working capital are particularly high in the distributive sector, which does not issue bonds extensively.[3] Two industry groups that appear in commercial loans but not in bonds are construction and mining. The latter, which includes oil and gas extraction but not refining (reported under manufacturing), was a growing share of total bank lending in the 1972-1982 period, partly as a result of the two oil-price shocks. In sum, a distinctly *broader assortment* of industries borrow, and borrow fairly regularly, in the form of short-term bank loans than borrow in the form of long-term financing in corporate bonds.

A further method of contrasting these two types of corporate financing becomes available if charts are prepared that trace, for each of the two instruments, the dollar volume issued and the average rate of interest. Figure 5.1 presents data collected by the Federal Reserve from its quarterly Survey of Terms of Bank Lending (STBL), which was described and employed in Chapters 2 and 3, on the weighted average interest rates on new C+I short-term loans---those of less than one year---made by commercial banks in the quarterly survey period.[4] The other line on the chart plots the total volume of those loans made. Although it would be desirable to have both variables cover all twenty-one years 1970-1990 in this chart and Figure 5.2, the dollar volume in this one commences with 1977, since before that year statistics on volume were not collected by the survey.

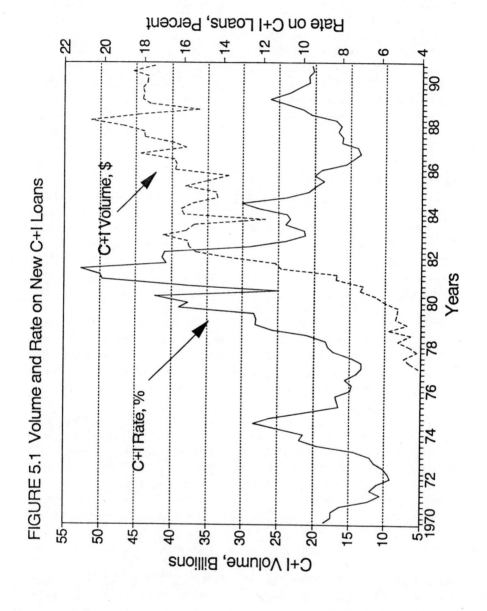

FIGURE 5.1 Volume and Rate on New C+I Loans

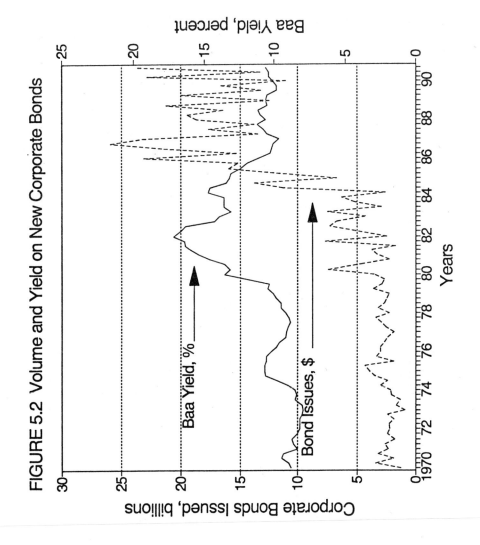

FIGURE 5.2 Volume and Yield on New Corporate Bonds

In Figure 5.2 are shown the dollar volume and average yield of new corporate bonds issued over the years 1970-1990, employing not only the same time period but also the same scale for dollar volume, in billions, and the same scale for the interest rate as used on the left and right vertical scales, respectively, for Figure 5.1. Numbers for dollar amount are those compiled by IDD Information Services, Inc. and the Federal Reserve at present and, before 1989, by the Securities and Exchange Commission. For the chart, the amount reported in the same four quarterly months represented in the STBL for bank C+I loans have been used for charting the bond volume and yield. Decision as to which bond interest series to choose was reached after some experimentation, as well as consultation with experts in that field. Since the volume series available refers to total bonds of all grade-ratings, the problem was to select a published rate that would be representative of the quality of the "average" bond, and would be roughly comparable with the typical or modal quality of C+I loans. The consensus reached was fairly firm for choosing the Baa grade bond-rate series as computed by Moody's Investors Service.[5]

These two charts, taken singly and taken in juxtaposition, provide some interesting behavior patterns, some of which confirm the generalizations reached by economic theorists. Variation in the level of the interest rate on short-term bank loans to business firms is seen to be marked and frequent *per se*, as well as in comparison with the gentler movements of the bond rates. This conforms with the findings of the relatively few economists who have accorded theoretical attention to short-term rates. Bankers and business economists have, on another point about level, long held the conviction that, for a family of bonds, the yield curve across maturities typically rises in direct relation to maturity length. For our two interest-rate series from dissimilar markets, that observation holds true more often than not, though with numerous exceptions. If compared on an annual basis rather than quarterly, the annual average yield on grade Baa bonds during the 20 years 1950-1969 was higher than the C+I new loan rate in 12 of those years and lower in 8. For the 21 years 1970-1990, the bond rate lay above the C+I rate in 15 of the 21 years, and lower in 6.

When attention is turned from the relative movements and position of the interest rates to the behavior of *volume* in the two markets, the differences are found to be still greater. Both bond issuance and bank-loan issuance (for the years that the latter can be judged) were at low levels in the 1970s. In fact, corporate bond flotations varied narrowly in the range of $2-5 billion per quarter from 1970-1982. In the following year, the amount of bond issues moved out of that band and pursued a set of jagged fluctuations that spiked briefly in the first quarter of 1987 at about $26 billion before dropping back sharply. Thereafter, the volume fluctuated markedly in the $10-17 billion level. In contrast, new C+I loan volume rose at moderate pace in 1977 through 1979, and then took off briskly from about the $8 billion level on an almost unbroken climb to $38-40 billion in 1982-1983. After that, the slope of the rise was lower and more erratic, but still slightly upward.

Examination of the respective paths of the interest curve and the volume curve, as well as the relationship between these two lines, thus shows relatively little similarity in price-quantity behavior between the bond and the short-term bank loan. Earlier in this chapter we have reviewed evidence that these two credit markets differ in the composition of industries that borrow in their respective loan instruments, and also differ in the regularity of such borrowing. These two separate bodies of data, taken together, seem to corroborate the tenet of economic theory that the long-term capital market differs in character and economic role from short-term lending. Therefore, there is no reason to expect that conclusions reached by economic theorists about the long-term bond---whether correct or incorrect in that context---should necessarily apply to short-term bank loans to business firms. Indeed, those authors themselves stated, for example, that in the latter market the rates of interest are set momentarily by transitory influences not related to the rate of return on physical capital. Bond prices and interest rates are determined by auction in organized securities markets.

In the last few pages, the discussion of Figure 5.1 was concerned with identifying the similarities or difference between the bond market and the C+I bank loans as to the path of interest rates and volume of loans issued. It is instructive to return now to Figure 5.1 in order to examine it from another stand-point. This chart depicts the volume and average rate of interest on short-term C+I bank loans over the period 1970-1990. In standardized terminology, the curves present separately the quantity and average price, recorded quarterly, in a specified sectoral market over a stated period. The two lines do not, of course, constitute the demand curve and supply curve of conventional analysis that apply to a given single moment in time. But what, if anything, are these lines able to indicate, either separately or in relation to each other, about operations in this market during the period?

In the first 5-5½ years covered by the series on dollar volume, the amount climbed rapidly, culminating in a brief peak in mid-1983. It then dropped sharply for three quarters before resuming a rise at a more moderate, but zig-zag, pace through 1990. The course of the average interest rate began a steep rise in 1977 closely paralleling the slope of the volume line, though reaching a peak more than a year before the latter, in late 1981-early 1982. From then on, average interest rates fell steeply through 1982-1983 before assuming a much more gradual declining direction, followed by a return to the 8-10 percent level for the years 1988-1990. In short, during the fourteen years for which both volume and interest figures are available, the two curves paralleled each other upward for roughly the first half of the period and then took generally opposite directions for the second half. If we look at Figure 5.1 in the expectation of gaining a clear, unified picture of the period covered---an integral *Gestalt*---it is not forthcoming.

More plausible does the result appear if we visualize a perpendicular line dividing the period of time into two parts, with the division made approximately somewhere in 1981. Looked at separately in this way, the first half would show the rate on business loans and the volume lent both moving rather constantly upward in parallel fashion; and the second half would present a less uniform but broadly continuing picture of the two curves varying in opposite directions. Whether either half could be satisfactorily explained by factors endogenous to the banking industry itself or to the short-term loan market in general, or by factors external would remain to be established. Other empirical material to be explored later in this chapter and the following one may shed some additional light to aid the analysis. At the present stage, one is limited to saying that the two variables in Figure 5.1 do not seem to offer, by themselves alone, a coherent explanation of the short-term loan price determination.

Interest Movements Relative to Current Prices

Throughout the twentieth century, there appears to have been a consensus among economists that an upward movement in the general price level usually is accompanied by a concurrent increase in the interest rate on long-term bonds. The same concomitance of direction between the two variables has been held to apply also to downward movements, though these are less frequently discussed. This relationship between the rate on capital loans and the general price level occupied a prominent place in Wicksell's theory of the manner through which a divergence between the present bond rate (his "market rate") and the normative "natural" rate tends to be narrowed by a cumulative process of successive forces. It was held that under full employment of resources and other assumptions, if additional money is injected into the economic system at a time when the market rate lies below the idealized natural rate, the bond rate will temporarily decline further, inducing an increase of borrowing, of investment, of prices for capital (producers') goods, and, as total demand is thus expanding, of prices in general. This chain of developments would soon restore the market rate for bonds to its former level and even nudge it higher toward the natural rate on long-term capital formation.

Concurrence between the movements of interest rates and general prices does not rest for all economists, of course, on an adherence to the notion of an equilibrating mechanism linking actual rates to a modeled "natural" rate. Even Wicksell described several different circumstances under which, for a time, both general prices and the loan price may be changing in the same direction.[6] Either of the series could be the first to commence moving; but the factors bearing upon prices are considered to accord the generative or causal role usually to the price side.

Price statistics presented in Figure 5.3 provide an opportunity to examine the pattern of price fluctuations relative to C+I interest-rate fluctuations in the years 1950-1990. In addition to the familiar curve on the annual weighted average C+I loan rate at large banks, the chart includes two broadly-based measures of changes in average prices. The first of these is the implicit GNP price deflator, the index that represents the price component in the official estimates of the nation's gross national product published quarterly by the Bureau of Economic Analysis of the U.S. Department of Commerce. For analysis in conjunction with data concerned with bank loans made to nonfinancial corporate firms across the wide spectrum of industrial groups that are the short-term borrowers at banks (as demonstrated in Table 5.1), the series on changes in the implicit GNP price deflator constitutes the most relevant measure of *changes* in general prices. The other price indicator charted is the Bureau of Labor Statistic's index of year-to-year changes in prices paid by urban consumers (the CPI). Although the components of this index are primarily prices paid by individuals and households for retail purchases of goods and services, and these households manifestly are not direct participants as borrowers in either the bond market or the C+I loan market, the corporate firms that borrow in those two markets are engaged in the production of goods and services that ultimately reach household

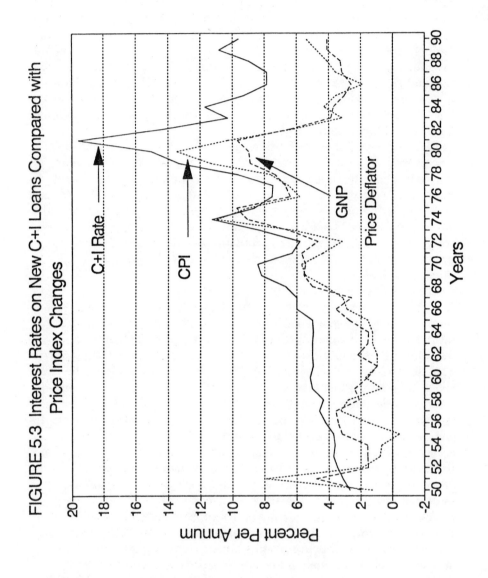

FIGURE 5.3 Interest Rates on New C+I Loans Compared with Price Index Changes

consumers, whose consumption accounts typically for 66-67 percent of the U.S. gross national product.

The decade of the 1950s was one of low but fairly steady growth of output accompanied by price levels that were less stable than production, but which nevertheless rose moderately, between 1.5 and 3.0 percent per year---with the exception of 1951, in which both of the price indexes in Figure 5.1 rose sharply. In the 1960s, the price movements continued to be modest, and the stability of the C+I loan rate was remarkable from the late 50s to the late 60s. Both prices and the business loan rate then began a more rapid pace of increase that lasted throughout the 1970s, and by 1972 the margin between the price curves and the loan rate had narrowed greatly. During many of the years 1950-1980 a rise in the price level preceded that of the interest rate, and typically the swings were wider.

The year-to-year price increases during the 1970s and the levels of the average C+I rate were very close through 1978, after which the GNP deflator slowed its rise. Changes in consumer prices kept pace with the mounting business-loan rate from 1978 through 1980, but then turned sharply downward and caught up with the drop in the GNP price-change index. Although the C+I rate, starting from its 1981 peak of nearly 20 percent, declined each year (with one exception) until 1986, the spread between the bank-loan rate and the two measures of inflation had widened substantially in 1980-1981, and the spread persisted at about 6 percentage points up to 1990. The three periods on Figure 5.3 that exhibit steep declines in the three curves---1971-1972, 1975-1976, and 1982-1983---roughly coincided with the recessionary state of the economy in those periods.

One observes that during the 40 years under scrutiny, there was one stretch of almost ten years within which the short-term C+I interest curve was virtually flat: from 1957 to 1966. This behavior occurred during a period in which yearly changes in both of the two price series registered changes that hovered around 2 percent per year. There were no other similar relationships in the 40-year period; and the years before 1950 are scarcely comparable, owing to special conditions that prevailed in the Great Depression and in World War II and its aftermath. No conclusion should be drawn from this single instance, even if one were convinced that short-term interest movements are fully determined by current changes in general prices. But it may suggest the possibility that, to the extent that changes in broad-based price indices are one factor that can, under some conditions, influence bank lending rates, there may be a minimum-sensitive price change below which that influence on short-term interest rates may be negligible.

Measured by the series on average annual yields on grade Baa corporate bonds, the interest return on these bonds fluctuated quite narrowly in the 1950s and much of the 1960s. Moreover, for the years from 1954 (the beginning of the Baa data series) through 1968, these yields roughly resembled the annual average rates on C+I bank loans, but that resemblance greatly diminished in the years 1970-1990. From 1969 to 1979, the bond series showed an upward movement the slope of which roughly matched the trend in price changes, though the latter were more irregular (Figure 5.4). Baa bond yields hit their peak of 16 percent in 1980 and 1981, and their descent from those figures has been slow, reaching a level just over 10 percent in 1989 and 1990. Changes of direction as well as increases in the slope of the price curves tended to precede those movements in the bond yields.

Possible Impact of Expected Price Change

Near the end of Chapter 4, mention was made of the argument, advanced by Fisher and some followers, that an increase in the public's expectation about the level of future prices will have a prompt effect on raising the level of *current* prices by the same percentage change. The time-phasing of this hypothetical process seems to embrace both an expected rise of the price level at, say, one year hence, and the rapid impact of that change in expectation backward onto today'sprices and interest rates, without any changes in relative prices or the level of activity.

The author would have liked to test this theory by empirical means. Unfortunately, a search of the probable and potential information sources has been fruitless; namely, there are no statistical data on future price levels for the United States that are useable for this exercise. Brushing aside conceptual problems, such as the improbability that at any given day or week there is any *generally-held* projection of where the price level will be in twelve months' time, the author explored various sources of what might be relevant data. Officials in U.S. government agencies specializing in price statistics confirmed that none of those agencies has compiled an index of projected future prices. One source that does exist is a private organization that, utilizing quotations on commodity futures, has published for more than a decade an index consisting of an unweighted geometric average of daily closing prices of 21 commodity futures (in 1988 the number was 27). Of the 21 components, 15 are

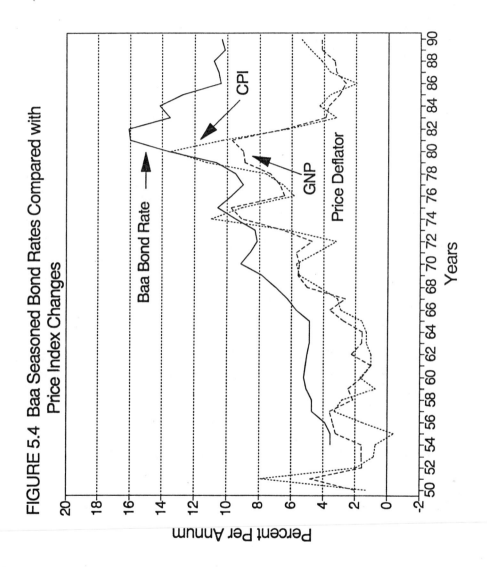

FIGURE 5.4 Baa Seasoned Bond Rates Compared with Price Index Changes

agricultural raw or partially-processed materials; the other six are heating oil, lumber, copper, gold, platinum, and silver.[7]

Apart from the fact that the index's composition is not sufficiently representative, even of the field of basic materials, a comparison of this index of futures with available series on commodity spot prices shows a similarity that suggests the possibility that futures quotations may mainly constitute present market prices plus an allowance for carrying costs, rather than the accurate, powerful foresight that Fisher ascribed. While the present author does not doubt that individuals and groups in one sector or another do form estimates of what prices in their respective sectors are likely to be at some future date, the identity of those sectoral items and the future dates pertinent to forward estimation must vary considerably across industrial and household sectors. In periods of persisting inflation, the public may count on a continuation of rising prices; but, as the preceding chapter brought out, the stickiness of some prices and volatility of others, together with other important departures from the Fisherian assumptions about markets, prevent an increase of inflation (or expected increase) from producing only benign and uniform macroeconomic effects, with no change in relative positions. If the required data did exist, they probably would offer little confirmation of the neutral-impact theory.[8]

Recent Empirical Studies on Interest

At this point in the chapter, it seems opportune to interrupt temporarily the presentation of statistical material prepared specifically for this study on short-term commercial and industrial loans by banks, in order to summarize some of the pertinent empirical research performed in this field by others. Altogether, the total amount of work that has been devoted to numerical measurement in this area, as well as the diversity of approach and sophistication, are huge. Much of the material is not relevant to the focus of this book, and other portions of past studies are out of date, or otherwise superseded, in their own special areas. This resume will refer to findings that may be relevant here.

Statistical research devoted to the subject of interest and interest rates had its serious beginnings in the latter part of the nineteenth century, and usually exhibited three common attributes. For the most part, the early empirical studies were undertaken by economists concerned with capital theory (and sometimes with business cycles), who were seeking to verify and enhance theoretical propositions.

Second, the interest-rate data collected and analyzed referred to long-term rates in the corporate and government bond markets. And the orientation tended to emphasize the relation of those rates to other variables, notably movements in the general price level and in investment. Typical examples of the empirical research accomplished in the late-nineteenth and early-twentieth-century period are found among the works of Wicksell, Davidson, Tooke, Jevons, Fisher, and Lutz as referred to in Chapter 4.

The three attributes mentioned in the preceding paragraph continued to characterize the empirical approach to the study of interest rates into the second half of the twentieth century; but at the same time the analytic motivation became more focused, and the technical capabilities improved. As for the latter developments, they resulted from the rapid proliferation of statistical data collected on a periodic basis by governments, central banks, and private research bodies; technological advances in machine methods to store and manipulate these data; and other related and familiar changes. The intensified analytic motivation to reach out for empirical verification of economic theories of interest, on the other hand, is much less familiar or understood than the electronic revolution. By the early 1950s, interest-rate theory had evolved to the point of acknowledging the existence and credibility of two main theoretical constructs in regard to how interest rates (for long-term capital loans) are determined---the loanable funds and liquidity preference theories. Moreover, some economists well-versed in the field concerned were expressing the view that the differences between those two versions were more a matter of formulation than of essence. Whether considered as basically integral or distinct, they resemble each other to the empiricist since, as pointed out in Chapter 4, he is confronted in either case with the concept of a demand curve and a supply curve, each of which is highly aggregative of components that are known to be numerous but are largely only imperfectly identified.

This poses the problem for the empirical researcher of choosing whether to accept the fact that the demand and supply curves for "loanable funds", as hitherto formulated, are unpenetrated, and perhaps presently impenetrable, composite schedules. In that event, perhaps the indicated approach is to attempt to identify the shape and level of each of the two composite curves at a given statistical "day", and at periodic days. That course, if it is to succeed at all, is probably more plausible the more one aims at finding, and being satisfied with, something called "the" interest rate in the neoclassical and Keynesian systems.

A much different approach to the one above was adopted by the leaders of a long-term research program that was started at the beginning of the 1960s by the National Bureau of Economic Research, with the support of the American Council of Life Insurance, and continued its carefully planned work some eighteen years. While expressing the hope that empirical research ultimately might assist in discovering and interpreting the composite demand and supply curves of the interest-rate scholars, the program directors felt that arriving at that goal would require also "detailed observation of the real-world elements" that lie behind the simple model.[9] A basic decision taken was to launch an avowedly disaggregative program of individual studies, but ones coordinated by the leading participants. The main goals were to observe the behavior in a fairly widely chosen list of rates over a long time; to compare the observed movements with cyclical fluctuations of "general business" (definition not published, to this author's knowledge); and to relate the findings to other studies bearing on interest rates generally.[10]

The procedures and tentative findings of the National Bureau of Economic Research (NBER) that are pertinent to this book are not those addressed---like virtually all previous research---to interest rates on government securities or corporate bonds, or to the term-structure of securitized instruments, but a few sections dealing with short-term instruments. These occur mainly in the course of an extensive NBER study by Cagan on cyclical movements of interest rates over periods from various starting dates through 1960. Particular attention was directed at the two questions of timing and amplitude. On *timing*, the NBER paper confirmed earlier observation that variation in long-term rates had typically lagged behind the business cycle at its peak and especially at its trough in the early years of the century; but that the extent of the lag had later declined steadily. By the end of 1960, the lags of interest rates at cyclical troughs still exceeded instances of leads, but at peak points in cycles long-term rates had caught up and in some cases led other cyclical series.

Five short-term instruments were also examined in the Cagan paper on cycles: Treasury bills, call money, commercial paper, bankers' acceptances, and "bank loans" (although not defined, this last series must be the average interest rate on short-term business loans at large commercial banks, the principal series used in this book). Although these short rates had already been more synchronous in the business cycle swings than the long-term rates, they also grew closer in timing over the course of the study. Over the period from 1920 through the peak of 1960, the bank-loan rate tended to lag the business cycle somewhat more than the other four short rates, though at the 1960 peak all five short-term rates led the business cycle indicator. Cagan's findings indicate that, over the 1920-1960 period, at turning points the various interest-rate series tended to cluster more toward each other than to the business cycle.

With regard to *amplitude*, that term was used in this particular NBER exercise to mean amplitude per time unit---specifically, the average rise or fall (in basis points) of a series per month. While the results appear less clear than those on timing, they indicated that for short-term rates, including bank loans, the average rate of change per month increased relative to that of a non-interest business cycle series (industrial production) over the period covered.

As part of this same NBER study of cyclical movements, investigations were made of the relation between the behavior of interest rates and the money supply. Economists have long recognized that, generally speaking, interest rates fall when the growth rate of the money stock is increasing. Attempts in the past to develop empirical evidence on the more exact nature of this inverse relationship have sometimes been disappointing. The Cagan research had noted that lags of the money stock at a cyclical trough had often, though not always, been paralleled by lags of interest series. Further study discovered that a higher inverse correlation was found when interest-rate series were correlated with the *rate of change* of the money stock rather than with the money aggregate itself, which earlier researchers had used.[11]

The NBER research program, which comprised numerous lines of investigation, working papers, and reports by a coordinated group of researchers and advisors, is perhaps the most ambitious and sustained empirical program, to date, in the field of interest rates. Its findings as well as its focus are useful with regard to the securitized instruments in the corporate and government bond markets. In addition, it advanced the state of knowledge regarding the behavior of various segments of the financial market, alone and in comparison with nonfinancial variables, at selected stages of the business cycle---a subject on which the National Bureau's output and standing have been eminent. With respect to short-term interest rates, including the short-term C+I bank loan, its work labored under time-period limitations regarding institutional factors and particularly regarding data. That is, data utilized in the pertinent study concluded with 1960, and the series had started about 1920; and for good reasons the authors excluded the years from 1930 through 1951. Therefore, as they explained, their findings on changes in cyclical behavior were necessarily based only on comparisons between cycles in the 1920s and those in the 1950s.

In another instance of coordinated group support of research involving the interest field, Tanzi and his associates in the Fiscal Affairs Department of the International Monetary Fund produced a number of studies in the early 1980s, some of which are theoretical in approach and others highly econometric. The main focus common to all is on the various effects created in the world in which interest income and interest expense are subject to various tax treatments; and on the interaction between expectations, taxation, and interest rates. A large part of the content is devoted to examining the Fisher theory in this field and the degree of its applicability, or lack of it, to the real world. Attention is concentrated on bonds, Treasury bills, and other instruments of the auction markets, rather than bank loans.[12]

Relationship Between Economic Growth and Short-term Bank Rates

After having temporarily interrupted the presentation of statistical material prepared for this present book, in order to review some empirical work done by other writers, our survey of potentially pertinent relationships proceeds now to scan the course of gross national product during this period 1950-1990. The possible linkage of interest-rate variations to the overall growth rate of the economy has received comparatively meager attention from economists, whether theorists or their empirical colleagues.[13] This stands in surprising contrast to the exhaustive discussion and debate about the nature of possible connections between long-term interest rates and the general price level---either the level currently beheld or that foreseen in a collective vision. The lack of exploration of this question can be explained only partially. In the years before World War I, the sheer lack of comprehensive systems of national income and product accounts in many countries meant that aggregative measuring tools were not at hand. Another plausible explanation is that the assumptions implicit or expressed in the general-equilibrium approach to economic theory are not conducive to considerations involving growth.

Even though the meticulously-conducted research that is now being devoted in all modern economies to the estimation of national accounts may not yet have reached perfection within its own criteria, the GNP data are generally accepted as being the most inclusive data available for measuring an economy's overall growth. For the present investigation, a decision to look at the movement of interest rates in relation to changes in GNP appears a logical next step, namely, by introducing variables that embody a quantity component---either a quantitative aggregate alone (GNP in constant dollars) or a composite of price and quantity (GNP in current dollars).

In the accompanying Figure 5.5, the annual average interest rate on short-term commercial and industrial loans is charted together with two series on the annual percentage change in the U.S. gross national product from the preceding year. One series is in nominal (current) dollars, the other in constant (1982) dollars. The two opening years on the chart, 1950 and 1951, lay in the latter part of the post-World War II boom that embraced high levels of physical output along with a short burst of sharp price rises in 1951, as was noted in a preceding section. Once past those two years, the growth in national product fluctuated, in nominal terms, in the range between one and 6-7 percent through 1963. In some of those years the GNP figures in nominal dollars and in constant dollars were close together, for that was a period of low rates of price increase. Commencing in 1967, the growth of national product measured in nominal dollars began an extended rise that was unbroken until the early 1980s. The C+I loan rate, from the middle 1950s through 1967, hugged a fairly flat path around 5 percent before starting on a prolonged rise. Viewed over the whole thirty-year period after 1950, the rate on new C+I loans followed a course that lay between the highs and lows of the changes in nominal GNP on its upward trend right up to 1980. In most years, the growth of GNP from the preceding year's level tended to lead the interest-rate movement, usually by one year. This timing relationship, as well as that in amplitude, became less regular as the 1980s approached; and from 1979 through 1990 the interest-rate level remained consistently above the percentage changes in GNP growth.

The pattern depicted in Figure 5.5 manifests several intriguing conditions that seem to invite at least some further attention.

* The percentage growth of gross national product in the United States from one year to the next, during the period covered, is often large, and usually greater than the percentage changes in prices (shown in Figure 5.3). During the 1970s and 1980s, even GNP in constant dollars frequently recorded changes in the year-to-year growth rate of 5 percentage points or more. As for the timing at turning points, the GNP series tended to show a slightly more pronounced lead over the interest-rate then the price series had shown.

116

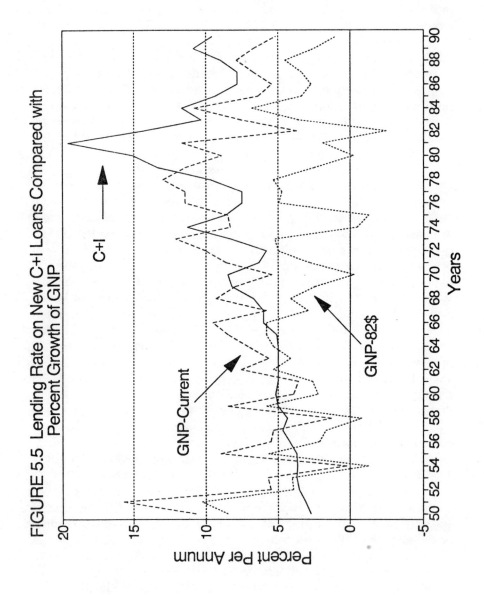

FIGURE 5.5 Lending Rate on New C+I Loans Compared with Percent Growth of GNP

* Although the two measures of GNP growth almost invariably coincided in direction at turning points, the spread between them widened substantially and steadily from 1967 through 1981, after which the margin decreased but did not disappear.

* As noted above, the course of the average interest rate on short-term business loans by banks exhibited a gently rising movement for the 17 years up to 1968, after which the swings were sharper and more frequent. Nevertheless, the trends of the C+I rate and the wider-fluctuating growth rate of GNP (in current dollars) climbed closely similar slopes throughout the period from 1950 through 1980. One feels tempted to draw a free-hand trend line through the two series, since the apparent rapport between them seems much closer than other suspected liaisons of the interest-rate that have been reported by economic theorists and examined here, such as its relation to movements in general prices or in the bond rate.

* Another fact that is inescapable is that the relationship between the short-term C+I rate and GNP growth experienced a major disjunction at or about 1981. Other charts presented here have displayed a similar discontinuity, if not rupture, and at the same period in time.

A later chapter will return to resume the discussion of this last-mentioned disjunction of 1981-1982; but the nature of the parallelism observed between the trend of the business loan rate and the growth of GNP can now be somewhat further explored here, statistically and analytically. To do that does not imply that the author has prejudged that one or the other of these two variables "determincs" the level of the other one. The decision to pursue simply recognizes the empirical fact that over a certain long period there was a similarity of movement that should be subjected to further measurement techniques, and recognizes the need to ascertain any logical basis for a linkage.

On the latter question, Chapter 4's review of the economic literature found that, although economic theorists as a group gave little attention to short-term lending by banks, some who did discuss it provide the elements for establishing an association between the movements of a country's aggregate value of output and income, on one hand, and movements in the terms and volume of the short-term instruments that constitute an important source of financing those fluctuations of national product and income, on the other hand. Writings of Hawtrey and Roosa cited in that chapter pointed out the interaction between the amount of bank credit extended and the terms involved, with sometimes one dominating, sometimes the other. They described the ways that, at times of cyclical peaks, some of the restraint was exercised by central bank action directly or through its signaling effect, and some by the commercial banks themselves, often by way of reducing credit availability in addition to tightening rates. They also stressed the greater sensitivity and volatility of short-term rates than long-term rates to those changing pressures. That contrast was also brought out by comparing the behavior of the bank and bond rates in Figures 5.1 and 5.2. Thus there is a presumptive logic in finding a closer similarity of short-term interest rates to the *volume* of GNP in current dollar terms than to current (or future) price indices, which have no quantitative content.

Since major economic variables can both influence and be influenced by other variables, further calculations were made to probe the relationship in the present case. In the course of these, certain experimental probes tried were discarded for insufficient theoretic or statistical value. Two that showed more potential usefulness for test purposes were to compute the ratio of the average short-term C+I interest rate in each year to the growth rate of GNP (in current dollars); and also the ratio of the *change* of the C+I rate from the preceding year to the growth rate of GNP just mentioned. The latter computation, while it produces tenable results in some years, becomes quite erratic for the latter two-thirds of the 40-year period (Figure 5.6). The other series generated, current C+I rate divided by growth of GNP, shows more stability than the one just mentioned, especially during the first three decades. For the whole period 1950-1990, the arithmetic average ratio of this interest rate to the percentage growth in GNP is 1.11, and the median value is 0.96. Half of the ratios in the series lie between 0.65 and 1.37. (In calculating the foregoing measurements and others in Table 5.3 and Figure 5.6, the freakish figure for 1954 is excluded.) The yearly deviations from the average ratio are depicted in Figure 5.7; and the average of such deviations, 1950-1990, is ±0.49. The relationship between the average rate on short-term C+I bank loans and the rate of GNP growth discussed in the preceding pages failed, on further examination, to demonstrate a unique and sufficiently stable relation. While the preliminary examination of the data had confirmed similar trends between the two data sets, subsequent analysis found the earlier indications insufficient. The arithmetic average ratio for the whole 1950-1990 period, is 1.11; and if the pre-1980 years are separated from the years 1980-1990 a better fit to each sub-period seemed to emerge. However, the calculated deviations from the mean, in either case, showed that the dispersion was unacceptably wide for predictive use. Indeed, tests of

TABLE 5.3 Mean Ratio of C+I Interest Rate to Growth of GNP and Deviations from Mean Ratio

	Ratio: C+I rate to % growth in current GNP	Deviation from mean ratio (1.11)		Ratio: C+I rate to % growth in current GNP	Deviation from mean ratio (1.11)
	(1)	(2)		(3)	(4)
1950	.25	-.86	1965	.59	-.52
1951	.2	-.91	1966	.63	-.48
1952	.63	-.48	1967	1.03	-.08
1953	.65	-.46	1968	.72	-.39
1954*	18.05*	16.94*	1969	1.03	-.08
1955	.41	-.7	1970	1.57	.46
1956	.76	-.35	1971	.73	-.38
1957	.87	-.24	1972	.58	-.53
1958	3.34	2.23	1973	.69	-.42
1959	.59	-.52	1974	1.36	.25
1960	1.32	.21	1975	1.02	-.09
1961	1.38	.27	1976	.65	-.46
1962	.66	-.45	1977	.64	-.47
1963	.89	-.22	1978	.74	-.37
1964	.7	-.41	1979	1.16	.05

(continued)

120

TABLE 5.3 (Cont'd) Mean Ratio of C+I Interest Rate to Growth of GNP and Deviations from Mean Ratio

	1950-1990		1970-1990	
	Ratio: C+I rate to % growth in current GNP	Deviation from mean ratio (1.11)	Ratio: C+I rate to % growth in current GNP	Deviation from mean ratio (1.11)
	(1)	(2)	(3)	(4)
1980	1.69	.58		
1981	1.67	.56		
1982	3.89	2.78		
1983	1.36	.25		
1984	1.08	-.03		
1985			1.46	.35
1986			1.45	.34
1987			1.17	.06
1988			1.14	.03
1989			1.62	.51
1990			1.92	.81

TOTAL Deviations: 19.64
AVERAGE Deviation: 0.49

Sub-periods
Mean ratio, 29 yrs. 1950-1979: 0.89[a]
Mean ratio, 11 yrs. 1980-1990: 1.68[a]

For the whole period 1950-1990:

Mean Ratio, 40 yrs. 1950-1990: 1.11[a]
Median: 0.96
Inter-quartile range: 0.65-1.37

* Year 1954 excluded from calculation of mean, median, etc.
a. Mean of columns 1 and 3 for years indicated.

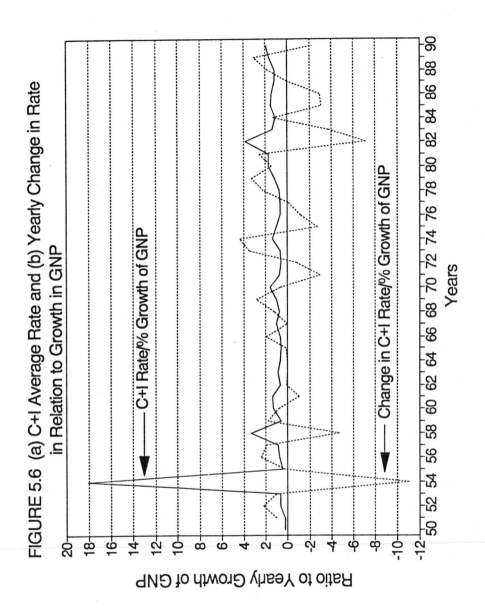

FIGURE 5.6 (a) C+I Average Rate and (b) Yearly Change in Rate in Relation to Growth in GNP

122

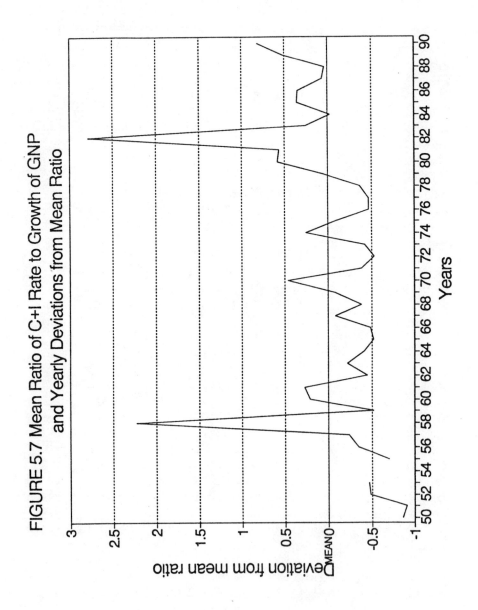

FIGURE 5.7 Mean Ratio of C+I Rate to Growth of GNP and Yearly Deviations from Mean Ratio

the statistical calculations, when applied to the years embraced in the study, yielded wide differences from the actuals.

One may conclude from this study that changes in the rate of GNP growth clearly do not constitute the unique "determinant" of the level of the short-term C+I interest rate. Certainly this is correct in the sense that there is not a stable statistical relation to the percentage growth of GNP that provides a reliable basis for projecting the C+I loan rate with any precision as to level or synchrony. The author believes that there is a relationship between the two variables, and that in a causal sense it runs *primarily* from gross national product to the price and volume of short-term credit. This is not meant, however, to negate or ignore the fact that when a palpable change occurs in the interest rate on this form of credit,which is employed by virtually all sectors of the economy, it creates effects upon prices and quantities in the commodities markets that, in turn, affect in some fashion the nation's gross product. This fact forms the basis of central-bank policy actions. Moreover, interaction is the essence of the macroeconomic process. A further reservation concerning the interest on business loans is that there appear to be additional forces, apart from changes in GNP, that exert some degree of influence on the level and movement of this interest rate.

Expected Profits and the Rates of Interest

In the course of reviewing what economic theory has said about interest rates and the manner in which they are set, we have encountered several hypotheses that run in terms of intertemporal effects. What these theories have in common is that each involves speculation about the power of some expected *future* development to affect, in some defined way, economic actions or events in the *present*. One of the best known and clearly articulated of these theories is that formulated by Fisher, who maintained that if a change occurs in the generally-held expectation about what the rate of inflation will be at a given future date, the effect will be to produce a prompt adjustment, by the same percentage, of the *current* price level and the current interest on bonds. This theory and the assumptions on which it rests were examined in Chapter 4 as well as earlier in the present chapter.

Although these theories have a certain amount of family resemblance, because they all emphasize some role to be played by expectations that link the present to a future time period, they differ in regard to their appraisal of the variables involved, the effects foreseen, and the reliability of the expectations. Fisher, for instance, believed in the universality and relative *certainty* of forecasting by all economic agents. "We need not ascribe to the practical man any knowledge of 'absolute' appreciation, but...it is included" in his forecast "of all the economic elements which concern him---prices for his product, cost of living, wages of his workmen, and so forth...His effort is not to predict the index numbers...but so to foresee his own economic future as to make reasonably correct decisions, and in particular to know what he is about when contracting a loan."[14]

In contrast to Fisher, Keynes's perception of how the economic system operates stresses the prevalence of *uncertainty*. From his earliest writings, there was an undercurrent of absorption with the relatively inadequate basis for projecting and decision-making and with the degree of uncertainty that persons attach to the projections they do make. Added to this perception was the realization, in his later works, of the lack of sufficient flexibility in the system to assure that equilibrium will be maintained at the level of full employment of resources. This preoccupation with the elements of uncertainty and inflexibility explains in large part Keynes's emphasis on the role played by changes in the public's preference for liquidity.[15]

While Fisher's faith in the accuracy of entrepreneurs' forecasting and in the comprehensiveness of the factors which the forecasts take into account is excessive, his views on this point do not differ basically from the views held---though less volubly expressed---by his neoclassical colleagues and classical forebears. Those writers stated that the rate of interest on long-term capital loans was governed, particularly on the demand side, by the expected net return on the investment in question. If one proceeds to enumerate all the items of cost and items of gross return that are involved in arriving at the net return expected, the list would resemble Fisher's list quoted above. In short, the investor-borrower of the classicists was presumed able to make , in advance, reliable estimates of the ultimate profits he would receive on his contemplated investment of today.

The neoclassical economists referred to above were expressing their theories in terms of the individual entrepreneur. If one desires to examine possible connections between the average interest rate on short-term bank loans and the profits or "returns" to be earned on the funds thus borrowed, what is pertinent is information on total profits in the economy. Statistical data are not available that can measure in advance a future profit rate, nor is there an index that measures what the public today *expects* the future rates of profits or of interest to be. What is possible in this area is to ascertain what the rates of profit have been in the recent past, though the process requires judicious decisions as to which data exist, or can be adjusted, to correspond to the purpose and sectors of the economy concerned.

Thanks to a welcome coincidence of timing, the author is able to utilize profit data that seem tailor-made for this chapter but have been compiled for a different research project by an experienced national-accounts economist, and made available by him.[16] The information presents the rates of return on domestic equity earned by U.S. nonfarm nonfinancial corporations over the period 1946-1989, which roughly conforms to the time span addressed here. Coverage of nonfinancial and nonfarm corporations is also compatible, since it corresponds to the population that constitutes the borrowers of C+I bank loans. Further details on the methods of calculation are given in the notes to this chapter.[17]

In Figure 5.8, three pertinent measurements relating to profits have been appropriately adjusted by Gorman to correspond to the coverage indicated above and to be internally consistent. Each of the three represents a valid method of measuring the average rate of return, but with different degrees of inclusion; and they are in the form of a ratio, in percent, of the profit total in question to the total value of the corporations' domestic equity. In all three cases, the profits figure incorporates inventory valuation and adjustment for capital consumption. The two lower curves obviously differ only as to whether tax payments have been deducted. The spread between the two upper curves results from the fact that the total corporate income includes the net amount of interest received, which has been deducted from total income to arrive at profits before tax.

During the whole of the period covered there were frequent and large fluctuations in the rate of profits before tax. For the long span from 1946 through 1969, the profit ratio fell below 9 percent in only one year, and in six of the years the ratio surpassed 13 percent. After 1970 the rate of return moved to a lower level, fluctuating mostly between about 9 percent and 6 percent, with a sharp descent in the early 1980s to a trough of 4-5 percent. The marked narrowing of the spread between the rate of corporate profits before tax as compared with profits after tax is attributable partly, of course, to legislative reduction of corporate income-tax rates and also to low levels of gross profits earned in some years, notably 1980 and 1982.

The preceding paragraph describes some of the main fluctuations as well as changes in trend of profits over the period since the end of the 1940s. The objective of examining those data is primarily to judge to what extent this information about the recent behavior of profits may have then enabled---or might now enable---firms in any given

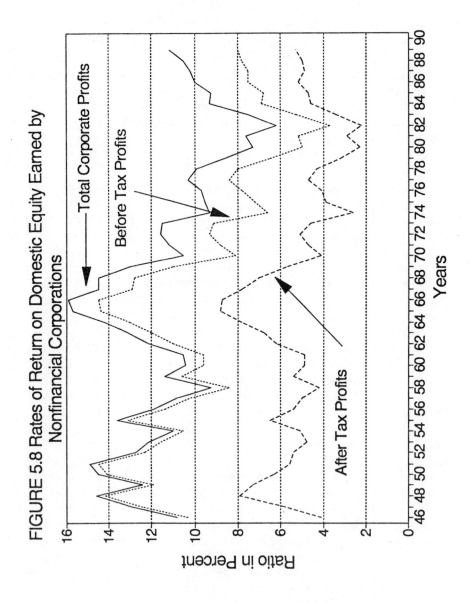

FIGURE 5.8 Rates of Return on Domestic Equity Earned by Nonfinancial Corporations

year to plan accurately their *next year's* levels of output, investment, and borrowing.   In order to facilitate what is, by any standard, a hazardous undertaking, a helpful step can be to look at the profit history in conjunction with the concurrent interest-rate history.

Accordingly, in Figure 5.9 the two relevant series on profit ratios---total income and profit before tax---are charted together with the average short-term C+I interest rate.   In contemplating the possible relationship between those variables, we can also bear in mind what was happening over the same time span in the behavior of price indices and gross national product.   During the years up to about 1968, the profit ratios were fluctuating in the high range of 10 to 14 percent, reaching their peak of somewhat above 14 percent in 1965 and 1966.   Over that same period to 1968, yearly price changes were in a zone from less than 2 to less than 4 percent, while GNP in constant prices was growing at a slightly higher pace than prices, and short-term bank interest rates were rising slowly from a level of about 3.75 toward 6 percent.   In brief, a period certainly not free of strains or excesses, but one of relative balance among macroeconomic forces compared with later periods.   It seems possible to surmise that if foresighted entrepreneurs in those years satisfied themselves that their projections of the prospective materials costs, wage rates, sales outlook, etc. for the coming year in their own respective branches would yield about the same net return as in the current year (perhaps with a glance also at the profit figures for the economy generally), they might well have concluded to continue or expand their levels of activity.

A different configuration of facts appears if the time is 1979 through 1983.   The average profit ratio before reckoning tax had declined in the mid-1970s to about 8 percent, and it sustained further successive drops to a record post-World War II low of 4 percent in 1982.   The national income and product was growing slowly and in two years was negative; and price increases remained high.   Lending rates at banks were rising at an even faster pace, peaking at over 19 percent in 1981; and by 1984 they were still at a level above the preceding thirty years.   Interest costs on borrowing by the nonfinancial corporations covered by these data undoubtably contributed something to the decline in their profit ratios in those years, as well as contributing to slowing markedly the pace of GNP growth and price advance.   In this instance, interest rates were acting as a causative force in affecting the macroeconomic stance---in addition to being influenced themselves, in the same and earlier stages, by the important price and GNP factors noted above and perhaps other factors.

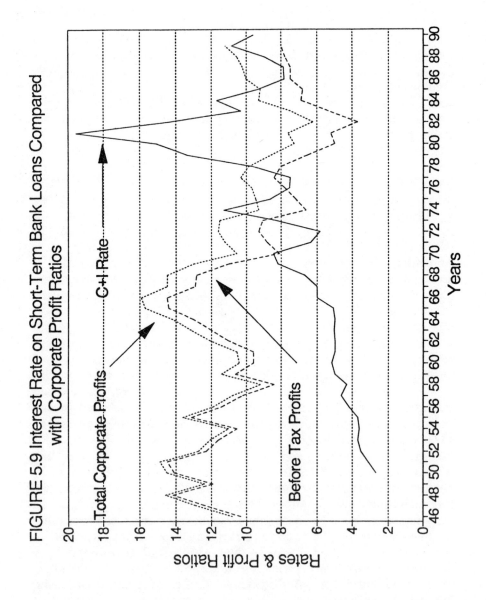

FIGURE 5.9 Interest Rate on Short-Term Bank Loans Compared with Corporate Profit Ratios

In the five years 1979-1983, conditions were sufficiently chaotic as to becloud the expectations even of entrepreneurs possessed of Fisherian foresight, as the low profit results of these years reflect. Speaking more broadly of all years, while obtaining a satisfactory net return is obviously a prime long-term objective for the firm, it is also the most difficult number to forecast accurately because of the many elements of which it is the net outcome. The theorists are correct in identifying its accuracy as the optimum goal. In the real world of less than perfect markets and of imperfect foresight, the firm may need---or even choose---for a time to forgo the maximum net return in favor of preserving its market share or some other consideration.

Summary Comments

The aim of this chapter has been to examine empirical studies in the economic literature relating to interest and the rates of interest, with the primary objective of ascertaining what they have found that supports or supplements or refutes the views and hypotheses of economic theory. Despite the paucity of attention devoted---by either theorists or empiricists---to the voluminous short-term lending by banks to commercial and industrial enterprises, a number of points have been found on which recent empirical research has succeeded in supplementing earlier findings or views of Fisher and others. Examples of this sort are developed by the author's research or identified here from work of other writers, including the following:

* Rates on short-term loans to business exhibit sharper and more frequent fluctuations than long-term rates.

* Interest rates on new C+I bank loans are usually, but not always, lower than rates on bonds newly issued or in secondary markets.

* In periods when the general price level is rising, the average C+I interest rate frequently also rises, though the timing and amplitude of the interest movements usually do not conform closely to those of relevant price series.

This chapter has taken note of the fact that economists from the dominant schools of economic thought have generally dismissed "market" (actual) interest rates from serious consideration, preferring to concentrate their analysis on some conceptualized "natural" or "normal" rate (Ricardo, Wicksell) or "neutral" rate (Keynes) which, under their adopted assumptions, would be consistent with maintaining the economy in equilibrium with stable prices (Wicksell) or in equilibrium with full employment (Keynes). Even for those who have addressed some analytic attention to actual rates contracted in the markets, the long-term bond and its yield are regarded as "the" loan instrument and loan pricing that have economic significance, and as substantively different from the short-term bank loan and its rate.

Though disagreeing completely on the bond's claim to sole significance, the author fully concurs that the two instruments differ in basic respects and have distinct roles. Evidence presented here has demonstrated that a decidedly broader assortment of industries borrow, and borrow regularly, in the form of short-term bank loans than borrow on long terms for capital formation by issuing bonds. On a different point, data over the period 1950-1990 show that the movement of the interest rate *relative* to the volume of loans made exhibited a very different pattern for new C+I bank loans than the pattern for new corporate bonds. The rate on bank loans also displayed a greater sensitivity to movements of major price indices than did the yield on Baa corporate bonds, and an even greater sensitivity to changes in the growth of GNP.

Moreover, basic operational differences exist in the pricing and marketing of the instruments. Bonds are issued in an auction procedure in which the relative forces of demand and supply determine the price and also distribute the issues among multiple bidder-lenders; they are securitized and are available for trading in an organized secondary market until their distant maturity. Short-term bank loans are arranged between the one borrower and, in most cases, one lending bank. Their discussion offers room for negotiation in some cases on the rate and other terms, but there is no auction among multiple parties. The bank loan instrument is not securitized; there are no daily quotations and no organized market, but individual C+I loans are sold in some cases by the originating bank, as described in Chapter 3.

We observed in Chapter 4 that some twentieth-century scholars, in writing about actual market interest rates, have abstained from the practice of attempting to discover and define in a few summary terms how a given type of interest rate is determined. The usual practice had perhaps unconsciously taken as point of departure the basic concept of binary opposing or balancing forces that underlie the discipline called economics in what Harrod terms "the basic axioms of statics": supply and demand, seller and buyer, lender and borrower. The two bare arms of supply and demand were then clothed, in the case of interest, with terms designed to be more specific to the subject. Those who have abstained from following that search for a few fundamental forces and collective expressions that may suffice in a commodity market seem to have found it more fruitful to regard an interest rate as an already going, moving phenomenon and to study the factors which at times move it or which it moves. This approach, while always a valid alternative, gains a firmer logic in those modern societies whose central banks pursue an active, discretionary monetary policy and whose governments recognize a responsibility in regard to the level of growth and use of resources. In any case, no new concise formulations of how the interest rates on short-term business loans are established have been developed in recent years, either by theoreticians or by economists utilizing empirical methods whose work was reviewed here.

This leaves an anomalous situation in which there is satisfied agreement in the economics profession that the rates of interest on long-term borrowing in the bond market are determined by an open auction procedure; whereas for the equally important short-term borrowing at banks there is common agreement only that those interest rates are *not* generated by auction, no consensus about what factors do govern the level and movement of the rates, and few attempts to improve the degree of knowledge on the question.

Notes

1. This series on large commercial banks' outstanding C+I loans, by industry group, was compiled by the Federal Reserve only during the years 1972-1982 inclusive.

2. In Table 5.1, the services industries group is listed separately but is also combined with trade and distribution, on the supposition that in Table 5.2 the group on "commercial and miscellaneous" must be the category in the bond list that embraces services. For Lines 1, 3, 4, and 5, the industry breakdowns of the two data sets seem to be more certainly comparable than Line 2.

3. See Hawtrey 1937, pp. 82-85.

4. The reader may recall that, as explained in Chapter 2, the STBL before 1977 surveyed only interest rates and only large commercial banks; thereafter, the survey covers both large banks and all banks, for interest rate and other data. When the average rate for large banks was plotted along with the average for all banks for the period 1977 to date, it was found that the parallel was so close that the large-bank series could confidently be used as a surrogate. This is advantageous, especially for use over a long span of years. That has been done in Figure 5.1, as well as other charts going back 20 and often 40

consecutive years.

5. A bond issue that is rated Baa is understood to be regarded as a medium-grade obligation that is neither highly protected nor poorly secured.

6. Wicksell 1898, pp. 165-168; and Wicksell 1906, Vol. II, pp. 183-190.

7. The index referred to is the CRB futures price index. See Commodity Research Bureau 1989.

8. For the Keynesian views about possible present impacts generated by a commonly-held expectation of a future price increase (formulated at a lower level of abstraction than Fisher's) see Keynes 1936, pp. 47-51 and 147-155; and Harrod 1973, pp. 73-75.

9. The quotation is from Conard 1966, pp. 6-8. Conard was a leading member of the NBER planning and analysis team, and his 1966 book, though not the last in the sequence of reports on the research program, probably best combines a presentation of the background and objectives with exposition of the tentative results.

10. Other references that the author has drawn upon in connection with the NBER program and other recent research include Cagan and Lipsey 1978, Guttentag 1971, Thorn 1976, Van Horne 1978, and Cagan 1972.

11. Conard 1966, pp. 65-66.

12. Tanzi 1984.

13. In the professional literature, references to the possible influence on interest rates exerted by changes in the rate of GNP growth are infrequent and usually sparse. This absence is noticeable, e.g., in at least the published reports on the large NBER research program such as Conard 1966 and Guttentag 1971, unless one counts the attention prominently paid to the timing of fluctuations in certain interest rates at turning points; but the orientation there is on short cyclical swings rather than secular growth. An exception to be noted is from the ubiquitous Fisher. In a chapter listing numerous factors tending to raise or lower "the" (long-term) interest rate---including such conditions as ethnic traits, scarcity of food, catastrophes---he adds some perspicacious paragraphs on the effect of a rapid rate of increase in the national income stream upon interest rates and investment. Fisher 1930, pp. 383-387; see also Koyck and Hooft-Welvaars, p. 243.

14. Fisher 1898, p. 378. Note a difference between the situation Fisher sketches here---in which each economic actor is regarded as trying to foresee those *selected* costs and receipts "which concern him" in "his own economic future"---and the situation cited earlier in which Fisher, in a different passage written at a higher level of abstraction from the real world, envisages the effects on the present of a *commonly-held* foresight by the *public* of a future change in the *general* price level.

15. See Keynes 1936, pp. 147-158, and the comments of Meltzer 1988, pp. 303-304.

16. The author thanks John A. Gorman, formerly a senior official in the Bureau of Economic Analysis, U.S. Department of Commerce, for permission to use the calculations and adjustments he developed to measure the rates of return for nonfarm nonfinancial corporations.

17. Statistical note: For the denominators of the rates of return, Mr. Gorman used Flow of Funds Accounts data as the basis for calculating domestic equity of the corporations, with adjustments to exclude income from corporate farms and to eliminate the components of net foreign direct investment. The numerators are Bureau of Economic Analysis numbers on income that incorporate the customary adjustments for inventory valuation and capital consumption.

6

The Bankers' View on Loan Pricing

"Call the first witness," said the King...When did you begin?"

The Hatter looked at the March Hare, who had followed him into the court..."Fourteenth of March, I *think* it was," he said.

"Fifteenth," said the March Hare.

"Sixteenth," said the Dormouse.

"Write that down," the King said to the jury; and the jury eagerly wrote down all three dates on their slates, and then added them all up, and reduced the answer to shillings and pence.

---Lewis Carroll, *Alice in Wonderland*

The preceding chapters have surveyed the subject of interest as seen by scholars who may differ to one degree or another, in substance or in method, but all of whose viewing-platforms are outside, far enough above the terrain to see it over-all, integrally—with scientific detachment.   Those economists whose approach is theoretical recognize, as might a medical researcher, that the economic corpus is a macro-anatomic whole, and they develop hypotheses about the active or reactive role of interest in the functioning or malfunctioning of the body economic.   Economists whose approach is empirical are the clinicians who apply tests and assemble data that can be totaled, averaged, and "regressed" statistically.   The findings of both schools have added substantially to knowledge about interest and interest rates and their relations to other organs of the economy.   This statement applies mainly to the behavior of long-term securitized loans and their auction pricing at time of issuance and in the secondary market.   As the preceding chapters brought out, however, for the important volume of short-term bank credit to business that is outstanding and is being replenished daily, our review has discovered no new and cogent explanation of what determines the rate on a new C+I loan and which factors govern changes in that rate over time.

If the findings of the scholars are less than satisfying, perhaps the search should proceed to other possible sources of opinion. An important and interested source should certainly be the banking industry itself, and this chapter will examine what the loan departments of U.S. commercial banks say about how the interest rates on commercial and industrial loans are arrived at, in their experience. Before proceeding to their domain, however, the tour should first stop briefly at the Federal Reserve. It is commonplace to give expression, both in the halls of monetary economists and in the financial press's columns, to the fact that the central bank in the United States and other advanced countries carries out its share of the responsibility to maintain economic stability and sustainable growth largely by measures that affect the volume of money and the rates of interest in the economy. In this process, does the Fed take direct action to set the specific lending rates at commercial banks?

The Fed's Authority and Aims on Specific Interest Rates

Let us recognize at once that the Board of Governors and the Open Market Committee of the Federal Reserve System do not have the legislative authority--or the appetite--for specifying the rate of interest that commercial banks under their jurisdiction may or must receive for C+I loans or any other type of loan instrument. It was not the intent of Congress to grant that type of authority to this new and first central bank for the United States when it was established in 1913, nor was that the desire of the main supporters and officials of the Federal Reserve itself. It is not necessary or relevant for this book to recount the origin and history of the Federal Reserve System. Suffice it to recall that the main objectives sought and pursued in the early years were modest, evolutionary ones that included harmonizing the regional disparities in banking services, providing a currency both national in scope and elastic, establishing a central "bank for bankers" to borrow from, and improving bank supervision.[1] By assuring this kind of framework offering banks a balance of benefits and obligations, the Federal Reserve could expect that interest rates on loans and deposits would be arrived at among the commercial banks and their customers by mutual competition in the marketplace.

In undertaking their new responsibilities, the Federal Reserve Board governors were careful and fairly explicit in matching their operating methods to their policy interpretation of the Federal Reserve Act. They conceived a main objective of the central bank to be to assure that a sufficient amount of credit would be available to meet the expanding "needs of trade"--a phrase that quickly became a slogan. Since quality was as important as quantity, the lending operations of each commercial bank should be based on actual manufacturing or commercial transactions of the borrower, evidenced by documents. Preferred instruments were bills of exchange or bankers' acceptances, since these were deemed best suited for use by the lending bank as collateral to borrow on, by rediscounting at its Reserve Bank. Thus, a commercial loan of high quality would protect the lending institution from credit risk, be eligible for discounting at the Fed, and help to finance the growing economy. The proper stance for the Federal Reserve, as thus envisioned, was mainly one of passive accommodation of loan demands from the nonfinancial sector, so long as they were sound individually; and the emphasis was on credit as the variable of concern rather than money. This initial approach to central banking was perhaps closer to microeconomic than macro.

In any case, it would not have been consistent with that ideological framework to mandate the Federal Reserve to set the interest rates on loans at commercial banks. Nevertheless, fifty-six years later, legislation was enacted by the Congress providing that "whenever the President determines that such action is necessary or appropriate for...preventing or controlling inflation generated by the extension of credit in an excessive volume", the President may authorize the Board of Governors to prescribe the maximum amount, maximum interest rate, and related terms on any loan. While detailed and sweeping in content, this Credit Control Act of 1969 was drafted clearly as a stand-by tool for use in emergency and for specified time only.[2] The sharp rise in short-term interest rates that had occurred in 1969 was destined to be more than doubled in 1980-1981. Pursuant to a decision and request from the President under the Act, the Board in early 1980 carried out certain temporary controls. In June 1982 the Credit Control Act expired, and was not re-enacted.

For completeness, brief mention should be made of three instances in which the Congress indeed acted to charge the Board of Governors with the duty to stipulate one or more of the terms applying to three designated types of bank operations, but *not* the commercial and industrial loan. These instances, which have the character of selective controls that have supplemented for varying lengths of time the general instruments of the Board's monetary policy controls, are briefly as follows:

(1) Interest-rate ceilings on time deposits. The Federal Reserve Act was amended in 1935 to direct the Board to set and regulate ceilings on the interest rates that banks could pay on savings deposits and time deposits. Under legislation enacted in 1980, these ceilings and the statutes requiring them were progressively abolished over a period ending in 1986.[3]

(2) Terms on consumer installment loans. During World War II and much of the following decade, legislation on consumer installment credit directed the Federal Reserve to devise and administer selective regulations on installment purchases of consumers' durable goods, for purposes of conserving scarce raw materials and reducing wage and price pressures in wartime. Control measures did not apply to interest rates but to the maximum loan maturity and minimum cash downpayment for different goods. These measures are no longer operative.

(3) Regulation of stock-purchase financing. Under the Securities Exchange Act of 1934, the Federal Reserve was authorized to regulate loans for the purchase or holding of stocks and convertible bonds. The purpose is to minimize the disruptive effects on individuals, the stock market, and the economy that can occur if securities are purchased extensively on borrowed money that is subject to call under changing conditions. The Fed's regulation takes the form of prescribing the maximum loan amount that a lender may accord on given securities. The difference between the loan amount and the purchase price is the borrower's "margin" that must be paid in cash. The Board does not stipulate or limit the rate of interest to be paid. In contrast to the two preceding examples of selective credit controls, this activity by the Board continues to be authorized and has fairly general public

support.[4]

In sum, the Federal Reserve governing bodies do not possess legal authority to set specific rates of interest (or maximum and minimum limits) on loans issues at commercial banks.   Moreover, the Fed obviously does not wish to exercise powers of this type, for quite understandable reasons. The serious difficulties that arose in the mid-1960s for the Fed, in administering the legislation mandating maximum rates for time and savings deposits, became progressively more severe throughout the 1970s, and ceilings were finally terminated by law, starting in the autumn of 1980.   That extended episode demonstrated, despite the good but misguided intentions of Congress in 1935, that distortions tend to be created when one important sector of prices is placed under administrative control while other prices are determined by free market forces. The Fed shares with a majority of the economics profession the view that the central bank's principal contribution to American macroeconomic policy continues to be its ability, enhanced by almost eighty years of continuous and sometimes faulted experience, to judge the appropriateness of interest levels and the money stock in relation both to the current situation in the money market and to longer-term requirements of the economy for maintaining sustainable growth.   Based on that judgement, the Fed uses its instruments of general monetary control to add to or reduce the aggregate reserves of the banking system.   That discretionary action in turn affects the *capability*--and ordinarily the inclination also--of banks and other institutions to increase or diminish their pace of credit extension.   In this dual process, various interest rates, including those charged and received at banks but others as well, re-adjust to each other as the altered monetary situation and other market influences may indicate.

Imperfect as the central bank's performance sometimes is, in strategy or execution or courage, the techniques for influencing interest-rate movements are more sophisticated and the effects more widely distributed than would be a regime of rate-fixing by the Fed.

Loan Pricing at Commercial Banks: A Self-Portrait

Among the purposes fulfilled by the quarterly Survey of Terms of Bank Lending (STBL) conducted by the Board of Governors, the primary one is to collect a standard set of comparable data on the total volume, number, maturities, rates of interest, etc. on newly-issued C+I loans, for use by the Board and the general public. As described in greater detail in Chapter 2, prior to 1977 the only statistic collected and published was the weighted-average rate of interest on short-term (up to one year) loans issued by *large* banks. From 1977 onward, the full set of items on business loans listed above has been published, and in roughly the same format and completeness, though with occasional changes in grouping or breakdowns. Beginning in August 1986, a new, non-numerical type of information was added to the reporting form, described as follows.

The reporting banks were now asked to specify the "most common base pricing rate" applied to the loans originated during the survey week in each one of the four maturity groups and sub-groups. This most common pricing base is defined as "that rate used to price the largest dollar volume of loans" issued by the respondent in the maturity group concerned.[5] The instructions pertaining to this item give the reporting bank a multiple choice for its reply, from among the following five designated choices: "the prime rate (sometimes referred to as a bank's 'basic' or 'reference' rate); the federal funds rate; domestic money market rates other than the federal funds rate; foreign money market rates; and other base rates not included in the foregoing classification."

From the introduction of this reporting item in August 1986 through the STBL survey week in November 1991, there have been only five and one-half years (22 quarters) of collecting experience. During this relatively short span, the answers supplied have registered a fairly high degree of uniformity—within each of the four maturity groups--across the 22 quarters. The rate on overnight loans was reported to be based most commonly on the federal funds rate in 21 of the 22 quarters. Loans for one month and under traced a more varied pattern. During the first 14 quarters, the majority of these short loans were priced on some "domestic money market rate" other than the fed funds rate; but in 1990 and 1991 the base was some unidentified "other" benchmark not included in the four specified rate types. For loans maturing in over one month and under a year the most common base was the bank's prime rate in 19 of the quarterly surveys, a foreign market rate in 2, and a domestic rate in one survey. Finally, among demand loans (loans having no stated date of maturity) the interest rate most frequently used as a base was the prime in all 22 quarters--though here, as in the other maturity groups, there was always a minority, larger or smaller, of loan transactions priced on one or the other of the designated choices. When all four groups are taken together, the prime rate comes out clearly in first place (Table 6.1).

In addition to presenting these results according to maturity groups, the STBL publishes the interest-rate figures and the pricing base distributed in a two-way breakdown between fixed-rate and floating-rate loans, by size classes. Placed on that basis, the predominant practice has been to use the prime rate as a reference point for variable-rate loans of all sizes. A high proportion of demand loans is booked at a variable rate "priced off the prime", and the same holds to a lesser extent for loans maturing between 1 and 12 months. A preponderance of overnight borrowings bears a fixed interest rate, expectedly, and is commonly based from the federal funds rate.

This voyage of inquiry into the Land of Interest has arrived at a point where, once again, it seems prudent to scrutinize the information or judgements reported in the present chapter and to appraise how these explanations relate to the corresponding views received previously from other sources. That fact that the Federal Reserve decided, after some consideration, to add the request that survey respondents indicate their pricing bases probably manifests that the Fed desired to pursue the thorny question of how short-term bank lending rates are determined.[6] And it simply regarded the STBL as a logical way of eliciting the desired information.

If we recapitulate briefly the received views on the above question examined prior to the present chapter, they can be characterized *grosso modo* as follows--to the extent that actual short-term interest rates were addressed at all. The neoclassical economists, who regarded short-term loans as rather uninteresting, unimportant, and transitory occurrences that are largely *ad hoc* and not subject to generalization, have explained these interest rates variously. To Mill, the interest rate

TABLE 6.1 Bank's Report on Benchmarks Most Commonly Used in Setting Interest Rates on Short-term Business Loans

Quarterly survey date	Total short-term	Type of Business Loan			
		Overnight	One month and under	Over 1 month and under 1 year	Demand
		Reference Rate Most Commonly Used			
08/1986	Prime	Fed funds	Domestic; prime	Prime; domestic	Prime; fed funds
11/1986	Fed funds	Fed funds	Domestic; prime	Prime; foreign	Prime; fed funds
02/1987	Fed funds	Fed funds	Domestic; prime	Prime; domestic	Prime; other
05/1987	Prime	Fed funds	Domestic; prime	Prime; other	Prime; other
08/1987	Fed funds	Fed funds	Domestic; prime	Foreign; prime	Prime; fed funds
11/1987	Prime	Fed funds	Domestic; prime	Prime; foreign	Prime; domestic
02/1988	Prime	Fed funds	Domestic; prime	Prime; foreign	Prime; domestic
05/1988	Prime	Fed funds	Domestic; prime	Prime; other	Prime; other
08/1988	Prime	Fed funds	Domestic	Foreign; prime	Prime; domestic
11/1988	Prime	Fed funds	Other	Domestic; prime	Prime; domestic
02/1989	Prime	Fed funds	Domestic	Prime; foreign	Prime; domestic
05/1989	Prime	Fed funds	Domestic; prime	Prime; other	Prime; domestic
08/1989	Prime	Fed funds	Domestic; other	Prime; other	Prime; domestic
11/1989	Prime	Other	Domestic	Prime; other	Prime; domestic

02/1990	Prime	Fed funds	Other; domestic	Prime; other	Prime; domestic
05/1990	Prime	Fed funds	Other; domestic	Prime; foreign	Prime; domestic
08/1990	Fed funds	Fed funds	Domestic	Prime; other	Prime; fed funds
11/1990	Prime	Fed funds	Other; domestic	Prime; other	Prime; other
02/1991	Prime	Fed funds	Other; foreign	Prime; other	Prime; other
05/1991	Prime	Fed funds	Other; prime	Prime; foreign	Prime; other
08/1991	Prime	Fed funds	Other; prime	Prime; other	Prime; other
11/1991	Prime	Fed funds	Other; prime	Prime; other	Prime; other
Summary of base most used:					
Prime	18	0	0	19	22
Fed funds	4	21	0	0	0
Domestic	0	0	14	1	0
Foreign	0	0	0	2	0
Other	0	1	8	0	0
Total, 1986-1991	22	22	22	22	22

Source: Quarterly reports of *Survey of Terms of Bank Lending.* Where two benchmarks appear for given date, second one is second-most common benchmark.

in the market is the rate that will equalize the demand for loans with the supply for them, in the same way in which demand and supply operate in any other product or service market.   To Wicksell, the market rate on actual loans is a price that depends on the momentary excess or scarcity of money.   Other authors (e.g., Lutz) went only so far as to declare what the rates on bank loans are *not*: they are not free-market rates. Ohlin went further than this, saying that for certain types of loans, including those made by banks, the pricing process is not amenable to demand-and-supply-curve analysis. For those loans, the rates of interest are fixed by the lenders, he wrote; but Ohlin then dropped the subject without attempting to decipher by what method the lenders set them. The Board's request for survey respondents to supply information on the bases they employ in pricing loans might, therefore, constitute an effort to pursue, consciously or not, the thought mentioned, but not followed through, by Ohlin.   For discussion purposes, we can examine separately each of the five optional responses that are open to the reporting commercial banks in the STBL.

Fed Funds Rate

This interest rate, otherwise known as the interbank loan rate, is the price charged when one commercial bank makes a temporary loan to another. Mechanically, this almost invariably is accomplished by an earmarking or other transfer from the lending bank's reserve account at the Federal Reserve Bank of its district to the reserve account of the borrowing bank. Hence, the term "federal funds", which is convenient shorthand usage, even though the money involved does not "belong" to the Federal Reserve nor is the transaction initiated by the Fed. As noted above, the STBL reported that the fed funds rate was stated to be the most common pricing base used on overnight loans from commercial banks to customers. As with the other reported pricing bases, no information is available as to whether the resulting overnight rate is above the fed funds rate or below. The more likely assumption is that it was above, since in some cases a bank will itself borrow in the fed funds market in order to grant an overnight loan. But in other cases a bank that is holding excess reserves could prefer to lend overnight at below the fed funds level rather than retain a partially idle balance.

Domestic Market Rate

This term does not attach to any single financial instrument. Instructions to the respondents simply refer to "domestic money market rates other than the federal funds rate." (Beginning with the February 1991 STBL release, the words "the prime rate and" were inserted, somewhat questionably, after the words "other than.") Some unidentified domestic rate--or perhaps several different ones--were reported as the most common pricing base for the loans of one month and under in 14 of the 22 quarterly surveys; and a domestic rate base was reported once each for the overnight and the over-one-month-and-less-than-a-year maturity groups. In the absence of more explicit information, one can only surmise *which* domestic base might have been used. Since the weighted-average maturity of the one-month-and-under group is typically 15-18 days, the choices might well include one of the current rates at banks' competitive lenders (1-month commercial paper; Fed discount rate) or rates paid by competitive borrowers (bank CDs or 3-month Treasury bills). This same short (under one month) maturity group reportedly used some different basing rate, in the catch-all "Other" option, in 8 of the 22 quarters.

Foreign rate

While this option was named as the most common reference rate only two times, both for the over-one-month group, it appeared a few times as the second-to-most frequent. The item concerned was undoubtably a current rate in the Euro-dollar market, such as the London interbank offering rate.

Other base

This category, apparently included in the STBL to capture any not-elsewhere-classified reference points or rates, was only reported as most common base rate in one maturity group: the 8 times listed in the under-one-month group. It was listed as next most common, however, 19 times among the demand loans and those with maturity under one year. It would have been more enlightening if respondents had been asked, whenever they had used some not-elsewhere-classified reference base, to specify what it was. Lacking that, one could surmise, for instance, that "Other" may in some cases refer to the reporting bank's own cost of funds, somehow defined; but that would be only conjectural.

Prime rate

The replies to the STBL question about loan pricing showed that demand loans had been consistently priced with reference to the reporting bank's prime rate (22 out of 22 quarters), and the maturity group one-month-to-one-year was not far behind (19 out of 22 quarters). Added to those maturity-group figures were numerous cases in which the use of the prime as a reference, though not the "most common" practice, was fairly frequent; e.g., variable-rate loans of different sizes and maturities. As a result, the cumulative outcome of the STBL for the 22 quarters showed that the prime rate was the most common pricing base for *all* short-term loans taken together. That fact, by itself, makes it advisable to scrutinize the prime lending rate carefully.

This majoritarian score is not the only reason, however, for examining the nature and habits of the prime rate, including its recent evolution. Standard definitions of this lending rate had appeared in diverse sources, but until recently they usually had exhibited a high degree of uniformity and brevity. A good example: "The prime rate is the rate that banks charge their most creditworthy business customers on short-term loans. It is the base from which rates charged on loans to other business customers are scaled upward."[7] Noteworthy is the clear association of this interest rate with lending to *business firms*, as distinct from other loan types. Each commercial bank maintains its own prime rate and changes it from time to time, but in addition the largest money-center banks formally "post" their rates. The announcement of a change by one of these leading banks is usually followed promptly by a move from other leaders, and a "national" prime rate quickly coalesces from this process, without necessarily producing identical rates at the smaller banks. In the period before the 1970s, movements in the prime were not frequent, and such changes usually displayed a lag behind cyclical indicators.[8] In that period prior to the early 1970s, typically about half of the dollar volume of short-term C+I loans made by large commercial banks bore the prime rate, while borrowing firms with lower credentials paid higher rates.

The Federal Reserve publication quoted in the preceding paragraph also stated quite candidly, "The criteria that borrowers must meet if they are to qualify as 'prime' cannot be precisely defined." That frank statement published in 1976 would also apply to the criteria employed today. What can be declared with certainty is that the role of the prime lending rate has changed in at least two respects, and that a shift has occurred in the center of gravity of the business loan rate-structure. These alterations progressed steadily, and some of them were nearing completion by the mid-1980s. Incidental to a change in the format and degree of detail in the STBL reports, the release began to present, starting in 1985, data on C+I "loans made below prime." From the first quarterly survey, for example, the new data reported that a total of $33.8 billion of new short-term business loans had been concluded, of which $26.1 billion bore a weighted-average effective rate *below* the prime rate. If one excludes the overnight loans (98 percent of which were priced below the prime), the remaining total volume is $18.7 billion, of which $11.2 billion, or 60 percent, carried an interest rate less than the prime. Data from subsequent surveys reported generally similar, large portions of the loans granted as being priced below the prime rate.

From the STBL reports as well as other substantiating information,[9] it becomes clear that the role played by the prime rate in the business-loan market changed dramatically in the few years between the mid-1970s and the early 1980s. No longer was it accurate to describe the prime as the favorably-low rate accorded to the banks' most creditworthy clients.[10] Borrowers with the requisite credentials are now able to borrow at an interest rate priced *down* from the prime or, in some cases, at a rate based directly on, or somewhat above, a given money-market rate. Thus, while the prime may not have become the ceiling in the architecture of the C+I short-term market, it no longer can be described as the floor. The weighted-average rate on short-term C+I loans--which of course comprises the relative weights of all loans, including those made at the prime rate--now lies *below* the prime rate since the early 1980s. Note also that the spread between the average rate and its heaviest component has narrowed, and narrowed more in relative (percentage) terms than in absolute basis-points, since the shift in the early 1980s described above. This seems to indicate an even greater (dollar) share of business loans being priced at or near the prime rate than in the earlier era (see Figure 6.1).

When one links this mutation in the *relative* level and role of the prime with the reported responses from the quarterly surveys, asserting that the "most common" reference base is the prime rate, one must conclude either that the prevailing position of the prime has moved upward or that the actual, contracted loan rates reportedly priced from the prime have moved downward. In either case, a shift in the center of gravity. Parenthetically, it is curious that although this

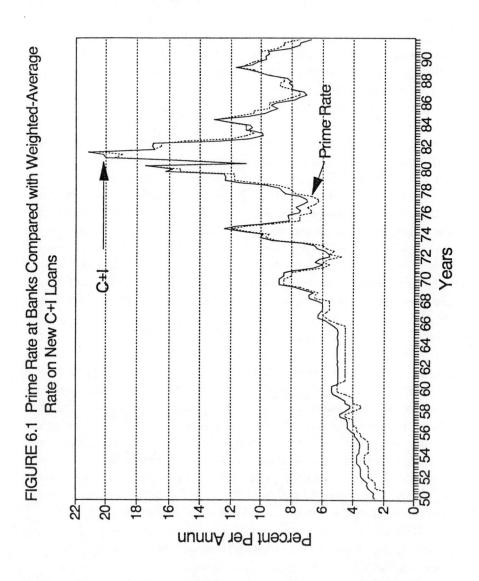

FIGURE 6.1 Prime Rate at Banks Compared with Weighted-Average Rate on New C+I Loans

mutation in the role of the prime rate was common knowledge within the banking industry, of course, and the STBL was regularly publishing various data about loans made below the prime, that fact and its implications escaped for several years the attention of many in the economics profession, the financial press, and some parts of the Federal Reserve itself.[11]

The other change in the role of the prime rate does not concern the business-loan field but mainly concerns some other types of bank lending. In recent years, mortgage loans, home-equity loans, or other consumer loans have been priced according to various formulae based on the prime bank rate or some alternative instrument such as a given Treasury security. Largely resulting from the belated conversion of some lenders and borrowers to the principle of the variable, or adjustable, interest-rate loan, and resulting also from enabling legislation that authorized depository institutions to make long-term loans collateralized by the uncommitted amount of one's equity in real estate, this method of setting the interest and other terms of long-term loans to consumers grew up quite rapidly in the late 1980s. Thus an interest rate that had been uniquely defined for and associated with short-term business loans--having now lost its original meaning and a part of its significance in the commercial loan market--finds its name and former prestige traded now largely in a different field.

Restatement and Preliminary Appraisal

This chapter opened with a short review of the powers and objectives of the Federal Reserve's governing bodies with regard to the short-term rates of interest on business loans. Despite often-implied or sometimes asserted views expressed in public debate or the press that the central bank has the power to fix the specific level of bank lending rates, the facts disprove that intimation or belief. The Fed has neither the statutory authority to establish interest rates by fiat nor the belief that it would be an effective and flexible method of implementing a sound monetary policy. Admittedly, the levels and rates of change of different variables, including interest rates, are indeed frequently the objectives of central bank policy; but they are pursued by applying a mix of general and sometimes indirect measures suitable to the current and prospective situation.

Interest rates on short-term money borrowed from banks by business firms must be determined by some method or combination of forces operating in or influencing the bank-loan market. We have consulted the information covering 22 quarterly surveys since mid-1986 in which the reporting banks state that they employed a certain base in setting the rate on their C+I loans of a given type. There seems to be no doubt or lack of confidence on the part of the Federal Reserve, which drafted the survey form, that these replies stated in terms of utilizing in some fashion a given base or reference rate adequately elucidate the process by which interest rates are generated on commercial bank loans. To the author's knowledge, the commercial banks also are satisfied with this explanation. Briefly stated, what the survey results declare on the subject is that the lending bank is the decision-maker. It chooses--among five permitted types of reference rate, most of which ostensibly lie outside the domestic banking industry--a reference rate as the base to which the bank will link, with or without some adjustment margin, the interest on a given category of business loan. Since these permitted choices leave much to be desired in terms of specificity, the replies are equally vague in identifying just what reference base was used and what adjustment was made to it. This drawback applies to the "domestic market rate," "foreign rate," and especially the "other" rate. Of the three just named, only the domestic-market choice was ranked as the most-common basing rate more than 2 times out of the 110 possible replies during the 22 quarters.

With those three last-named types of loan-pricing base necessarily excluded from further examination because of their vague identity and relative infrequency, the remaining types are the federal funds rate and the prime rate. These two interest rates, both of which rank high on the list of most-common pricing bases for C+I loans, differ widely from each other in nature and behavior. The federal funds market is a highly homogeneous and active market, displaying some characteristics of an auction, despite the fact that it operates merely by fast telephonic networks--without a trading floor and its appurtenances. This market is open to all depository institutions that benefit from the discount facilities as well as the reserve requirements of the Federal Reserve System, though its participants are mainly commercial banks. Some of them are lenders and borrowers by turn; other participants are habitual borrowers (mainly large city banks) or habitual lenders. Interbank loans in the fed funds market are predominantly overnight transactions, though often rolled over somewhat beyond that. As mentioned before in this volume, the two parties to a given interbank loan are typically a bank that temporarily holds some uncommitted (excess) reserves lending to a bank that is temporarily short of meeting the Fed's reserve requirements.

The volume of these extremely short-term transactions is customarily high,[12] but fluctuating, and the resulting interest rate on fed funds is correspondingly sensitive, changeful, and closely followed--for the additional and crucial reason that movements in the rate can reflect the current open-market operations of the Federal Reserve as well as the interbank transactions just described (Figure 6.2). Note that in the period 1954-1979 the average C+I rate was much less sensitive to economic downturn than the funds rate, owing partly to the lagging response of the banks' prime rate, whereas since 1980 the spread has been more constant cyclically. For the individual bank at any given moment, its marginal cost of borrowing additional money at short term is represented by a choice among the current fed funds rate, the Federal Reserve discount rate, and the bank's offering rate on short-term certificates of deposit. The CD rate is normally the highest of these alternative sources.

The fed funds rate and the three loan-pricing bases excluded above from this further examination are presumably all housed outside the domestic banking system. That is, they are interest rates generated to price some financial instrument (e.g., Treasury bill, commercial-paper note, Eurodollar) in a different market, whose participants have their own set of needs and criteria about loan terms that do not correspond to those in the C+I loan market. A partial exception is the fed funds rate where, as noted previously, the use to which it is put by banks in C+I lending broadly mirrors usage in the fed funds market itself, one stage earlier; in both cases, the maturities are very short and virtually identical, average loan sizes are quite large, and participants tend to be large firms also.

The prime rate, in contrast, is a distinctly different entity. A fundamental aspect of its nature is that it is essentially an "insider." As explained earlier in this chapter, the manner in which commercial

152

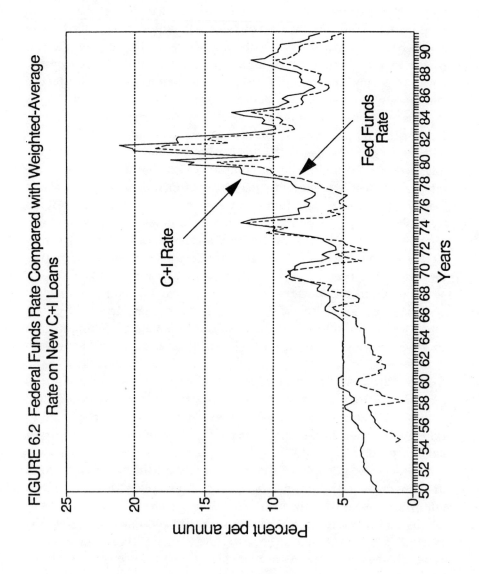

FIGURE 6.2 Federal Funds Rate Compared with Weighted-Average Rate on New C+I Loans

banks have employed the interest rate they call their *prime* changed markedly--virtually reversed--in the first half-dozen years of the 1980s. But it has always served as, and been described as, an internal benchmark or point of departure utilized by bank officers in pricing an individual new short-term business loan--mainly pricing somewhere below the prime rate since the mid-1980s, and mainly somewhere above the prime in the 40 years prior to that. When analyzing the survey results reporting that, for a given short-term C+I loan category, the most-common base used as a point of departure was the prime rate, one can wonder whether this represents some different or additional procedure, or whether it means that the reporting banks simply applied the same prime-with-adjustment procedure they always have done. The studies conducted in the 1960s, based on both statistical data and direct interviews, emphasized the diversity of criteria considered, especially by the large banks that exercise leadership, in agreeing to make a proposed C+I loan as well as in setting the interest and other terms. As a result, bankers confirmed, the C+I category of loans was the one within which the largest variety of interest rates was in effect. Some banks had formal rate structures for loans in this field, while others relied on a daily review; and "in either case the lending officer's judgement determined what rate should apply."[13] Wojnilower and Speagle also found that rivalry within a given bank and conjecture about potential reactions from competitors and customers helped explain the timing and amount of changes in the prime rate.[14]

When interest rates of all sorts soared to their highest peaks in the economic turmoil of 1980-1981, there was a brief revival of attention by some economists to the subject of rates on short-term bank loans, and the prime rate in particular. Since the process of role-transformation earlier described had started but was not complete, there was more confusion than clarity. Writers who managed to distinguish the more lasting aspects of this mutation from the transitional ones seemed to conclude that, so far as the nature of bank interest-rate determination is concerned, the complexity and imprecision have not materially changed.[15]

Ohlin, in a fleeting insight in 1937, had opined that interest rates on bank loans represented a pricing process not susceptible to fruitful explanation by conventional demand-and-supply-curves methods, and said that those loan rates are fixed by the lenders.[16] He did not elaborate; and the subject has largely been ignored by his contemporaries, as was noted in Chapter 4, except for occasional acknowledgements that bank loans do not bear an auction or free-market rate. Studies referred to in the present chapter, in addition to the question recently added to the Federal Reserve's quarterly survey, have produced further information on the nature of C+I loan pricing--in which the phenomenon of the prime rate plays a major part--and some of the factors and motives that underlie the pricing. The studies made in the 1960s pointed to conclusions that "leave little doubt that the prime rate is an administered price," characterized by rate changes initiated by a leading New York bank, quickly followed by a semi-collusive ratifying adoption by other big banks.[17] In more recent years, some large banks have experimented with their own, individual formulae or with looser forms of joint but not identical rate-setting methods that may lessen the degree of price leadership of individual banks. Fischer insists that "the prime by whatever name" and by whatever diverse and changing methods it is calculated continues to hold a cherished place in banking, despite the difficulty that bankers and economists have in identifying or defining it.[18]

The empirical, evidential summary that one receives appears to be that--apart from the very short-term, mainly overnight loans tied almost exclusively to the fed funds rate--the remaining short-term C+I loans are priced at an interest rate chosen by the lending bank and related in some changeful and circumstantial manner to the bank's prime rate (or set of prime rates) as benchmark. But there is no agreed or explicit theoretical or empirical exposition of how banks arrive at this benchmark rate itself.

In the chapter to follow, the author will explore a theory or process of business-loan pricing that has not been examined hitherto in this book, that does not occupy a prominent place in the literature, but that warrants scrutiny here.

Notes

1. For further information on Federal Reserve policy in the early period, cf. Chandler 1970, pp. 41-53; Goldenweiser 1951, pp. 110-130; Melton 1985, pp. 19-21; Kettl 1986, pp. 18-23.

2. See Board of Governors 1984, pp. 71-72; and especially Board of Governors, "Announcements: Monetary and Credit Actions", *Federal Reserve Bulletin*, April 1980, pp. 314-315.

3. See Brown 1987, pp. 1-11.

4. Young 1973, pp. 147-154; Board of Governors 1984, pp. 72-73.

5. The language quoted in this paragraph is from the Notes to the quarterly statistical release on the Federal Reserve's Survey of Terms of Bank Lending, Statistical Release E.2.

6. Brady's informative article, published in January 1985, stated that, "because the STBL does not collect information on base rates," a comparison he wished to make between recorded rates on two different maturity-groups would have to employ assumed rates and other estimates. About eighteen months later the STBL began collecting the pricing-base replies. Brady 1985, pp. 6-7.

7. Board of Governors 1976, p. 642.

8. Information on this process of effecting a change in the prime rate is summarized in Wojnilower and Speagle 1962, pp. 70-73. Hodgman 1963 provides an analysis in depth of commercial bank lending practices and policies, based partly on comprehensive interviews in three large U.S. money centers, in which the then-current role of the prime and bank strategies in lending occupy a central place. In his precise usage, the prime bank rate was conceived especially as the "minimum preferential lending rate to depositor-borrowers," though banks were almost as eager to lend to non-depositors. Hodgman, pp. 120-123.

9. Brady 1985; Polakoff and Budin 1973; U.S. Congress. House. Committee on Banking, Finance and Urban Affairs. Staff Report 1981; and Goldberg 1982, pp. 277-296.

10. Among Hodgman's findings was the fact that, even in the early 1960s, the criteria applied by large money-center banks in selecting loan terms for prospective prime borrowers were, in descending order, (1) deposit relationship, including the customer's compensating deposit balances that increase the bank's lending capacity; (2) credit rating of borrower; (3) criteria whose order varied with circumstances: contract rate of interest; purpose; maturity (short, seasonal loans preferred); pay-out schedule. In short, "creditworthy" involved more than the credit rating itself. Hodgman 1963, Chapter IV.

11. E.g., see International Monetary Fund. 1990. *International Financial Statistics*, June 1990, p. 555. Washington: International Monetary Fund. *The New Palgrave: A Dictionary of Economics.* 1987. John Eatwell, Murray Milgate, and Peter Newman, eds. p. 342. London: Macmillan Press Ltd. Board of Governors 1988. *Annual Statistical Digest 1987*, p. 242 (note Table 20). Washington: Board of Governors. All of the above repeat the definition of the original, but now-altered, employment of the prime rate in commercial bank lending to business firms.

12. There is no frequently-collected series on the volume of transactions in the federal funds market. Meulendyke quotes from data collected by the Federal Deposit Insurance Corporation on its quarterly call report covering all institutions that it insures, to the effect that those institutions' purchases of fed funds were running "around $145 billion" per day at the end of 1988. Meulendyke 1989, p. 73.

13. Hodgman 1963, p. 28.

14. Wojnilower and Speagle 1962, pp. 72-73.

15. Meulendyke 1989, pp. 59-61, 67-72.

16. Ohlin 1937; (see Chapter 4, note 50, above).

17. Hodgman 1963, p. 123. Hodgman then proceeds, however, to a searching, pro-and-con examination of the relative strength of administrative loan-pricing vs. interbank competition for lucrative prime customers, and the costs and benefits for borrowers, pp. 123-144.

18. "The prime is not a simple concept...It is multidimensional...In actuality, there is no other money market rate or composite of rates which could serve effectively as a proxy for prime...It is not a monolithic industry standard,...there may be local or regional primes, national primes, big and small customer primes," etc. Fischer 1982, pp. 12-13.

7

Creation and Evolution:
Further Views and Vistas

The main, direct influence of the Banking System is over the short-term rate of interest.

---John Maynard Keynes, *A Treatise on Money*

Interest is the most paradoxical of all economic questions...It is one of the main pillars of the claim of economics to be Queen of the Social Sciences, the only one of those sciences reducible to mathematical statement and analysis...Yet when examined closely, these claims dissolve.

---G.L.S. Shackle, *Economic Journal*, 1961

Contributions to systematic research in the field of interest rates have taken different forms and followed different approaches; and those approaches can be classified and contrasted in several different ways, as previous chapters have indicated. Examples of these differing and often competing treatments, which frequently coexist in pairs or threesomes, include the classical school vs. the demand-oriented marginalist school; the "natural rate" of interest embodied in the equilibrium model of neoclassical economics vs. actual market rates of interest in classical, Keynesian, or even more dynamically-oriented theories; hypothetical constructs in pure theory vs. empirical studies using inductive methods, etc. In all these alternative methods, the predominant attention has been focused on the long-term bond that is related to capital formation, is securitized, and whose interest rate and quantity are determined at auction in a manner conceptually compatible with the hypothesized demand and supply curves of traditional economic theory.

In the far less-explored field of short-term loans, we have noted the existence of a different pair of divergent contemporary approaches to the subject. One is aimed at developing a theory of how a given interest rate or set of rates is created or determined---which had been the major preoccupation in the study of "the" long-term rate in capital theory. The contrasting approach adopts the objective of regarding a given type of interest rate as a continuum or seamless web that is undergoing frequent, if irregular, influences that shape its development. Such influences can arise from events or forces generated in financial markets themselves or from exogenous sources---all so imaginatively listed by Fisher.[1] They can also be created or induced by discretionary actions taken by central bank authorities. This what-makes-rates-move approach is stimulated by the heightened degree of responsibility placed on governments and central banks in the post-World War II period for maintaining smooth, sustainable economic growth and employment, and by the not-unrelated desire of economists to increase the technical and policy potential of demand-management methods to fulfill that governmental responsibility.

Parallel to the just-named efforts, a modest but discernible revival has occurred, during the decade beginning in the early 1980s, of research directed again toward clarifying how interest rates on new bank loans are determined. The addition to the quarterly Survey of Terms of Bank Lending (STBL) of requests for information about the base or reference point used in setting the rate on each maturity-group of short-term loans is a major example of this type of renewed research focused on rate determination---in this case, stemming from the central bank itself. It does not escape one's notice that in this instance, as well as in the few other recent assays in the field, there is little mention of supply or demand curves---much less of sweeping abstractions such as Impatience or Liquidity Preference---and the name of choice is *pricing* rather than interest rate.

The manner in which the STBL question is phrased and the answers are reported reflects a tacit acceptance by the Fed surveyors of the proposition that there is a degree of *administered* price-setting in the C+I loan market. This fact is what was implied but not elaborated in the remarks, cited in Chapter 4, by Lutz that a commercial bank's lending rate is not a free-market rate, and by Ohlin that the rate on bank loans is fixed by the lenders.[2] In the case of the STBL also, the attributing of rate-setting to the lending banks has not been expounded in an explicit theoretical manner, but the inference can plainly be drawn.

The Fed's Venture into Mark-up Theory

The findings of the STBL with regard to loan pricing for different types of short-term C+I loans were cumulated, for the short span covered by these particular data, in Table 6.1 of the preceding chapter. Briefly stated, what these findings purport to convey is that for each *type* of loan based on maturity there can be identified a specific interest rate or other numerical benchmark that constitutes the most-commonly-used basis by banks for arriving at the interest-price on new loans of that type, though some other base may occasionally be substituted. The process thus portrayed seems to be describing a mark-up method of interest-rate determination. Generically, the term mark-up pricing as used in the wholesale or retail goods markets refers to a process of employing some selected price or other benchmark---ordinarily some cost element or composite cost incurred by the selling firm---and arriving at a selling price for the firm's product by adding to the benchmark an amount calculated to cover any remaining per-unit costs, including an allowance for profit.[3] Presumably, the STBL and its reporting banks envisage the loan rate-setting procedure as conforming substantially to the process just described. If the components entering into this marking-up are fairly stable over time, for a given bank, and if competitive conditions among banks tend to produce similar mark-ups across banks, tabulations of the comparative movements of the given base rate and the lending rate derived from it might show a sufficiently stable or consistent statistical relationship to confirm the reported pricing process.

The following paragraphs will summarize the result of an experiment carried out, along the lines just mentioned, to test the conformity of each of three different short-term C+I rate series with movements in its reported pricing base. Owing to the vagueness surrounding the reference bases of the other loan groups, this exercise must be confined to (a) the rate on overnight loans and (b) the two rates reportedly based predominantly on the prime rate.

Before presenting the results of this verification experiment, the author wishes to emphasize that, whether or not the STBL data may serve to establish a relationship between an actual average interest-rate series and the reference series that is sufficient to confirm the existence of a reasonably coherent mark-up pattern, the collecting of rate-basing responses has some value and validity. First, the data base embraced in the STBL is believed to be the only one of its kind and coverage that has been collected over an unbroken span on a periodic pattern.

Second, the decision to phrase the question on interest-rate setting exclusively in terms of a certain "base rate" chosen by the lending bank is a recognition---not always acknowledged in the past by bankers and economists---that interest rates on bank loans are not explainable in the general terms of the competing forces of demand and supply. (To take note of the Federal Reserve's forthrightness in that recognition, however, is not necessarily to approve the choices given to respondents and the manner of phrasing them, as mentioned earlier. In particular, not one of the multiple choices open to a reporting bank is a cost element or composite cost incurred by the bank on deposits or other borrowed funds.)

A third merit of the STBL's decision to approach interest-rate setting as possibly being a case of price fixing by the lending institution is that it serves as a link to scholars who see the process of setting rates at banks as involving a degree of administered pricing that places commercial banking among the many industries characterized by the hybrid market form of *monopolistic competition*. In addition to the observations of Hodgman noted in Chapter 6, the findings of Alhadeff, Chamberlin, Chandler, and Rousseas are germane in this connection.[4] We shall revert to this point later.

Owing to the degree of uniformity reported by the STBL in the banks' use of the federal funds rate as pricing base for setting the rate on overnight loans to customers, there is an empirical ground for expecting some stability in the latter rate's relation to the federal funds rate. In addition, there are the economic grounds previously stated for the same expectation. These run in terms of the liquidity of the funds market, its large volume, the familiarity of banks with its methods and movements through their own loans to or borrowings from that market; and even the fact that borrowed sums from the funds market are not subject to reserve requirements. A regression and correlation analysis carried out, using Planets software programs, with the fed funds rate as the independent variable yielded a correlation coefficient of 0.993. That result, taken together with the empirical and theoretical factors, seems to confirm a reasonably credible case for believing that the overnight loan rate to business firms is normally determined by a mark-up from the current fed funds rate. Whether this holds equally true both in instances in which the lending bank has itself obtained the money lent from this interbank loan market and in instances in which the money was lent from existing cash balances cannot be established from the foregoing information.

Testing the nature and stability of the two loan rates to business firms reportedly based predominantly on the prime rate appeared prospectively to be more problematic than the case of the overnight loan. The two C+I loan types under consideration are loans issued for more than one month but under one year, and demand loans (also known as those with no stated maturity). In both cases, the STBL respondents named the prime rate as the most commonly used pricing base, but in almost every quarterly report one or more other reference rates were also, if less frequently, used; and these latter, second-ranking benchmarks differed from time to time as between foreign interest rates, unspecified domestic market entities, and simply unidentified "other" rates. Each of these two loan series displayed additional types of variation over time. For instance, though both these loans were priced from the prime rate, they alternated between themselves as to which registered the higher weighted-average rate. The demand loans were predominantly issued with floating interest rates, and no information is available about the actual duration of these credits extended on a "demand" basis. The loans issued for a period of over one month but less than one year recorded an average maturity of 130-150 days; their breakdown between fixed and floating rates was much more evenly balanced than the demand loans, but the fixed-rate group was usually larger. In the mid- to late-1980s, the quarterly STBL reports showed that typically one-third to one -half of the loans in each of these two maturity groups were made at rates somewhere below prime.

Given the factors of variability exhibited in each of these two business loan types, and given also the lack of a generally-agreed viewpoint within the economic profession as to the nature and manner of determination of the prime rate itself, the prospect was not bright that regression analyses using the national prime rate as independent variable with each of the two series of actual weighted-average interest rates would produce results demonstrating a close and reliable relationship. In this exercise, the correlation coefficient in the case of the over one month/less than one year loan group was 0.964. For the demand loan group, the coefficient was somewhat higher at 0.977.

To recapitulate, this section examined the pricing methods reportedly employed by U.S. commercial banks in setting the interest rate on three groups of commercial and industrial loans. For the first of these, the stated basing of overnight loans to C+I borrowers upon the federal funds rate, the empirical data collected by the STBL corroborated the economic plausibility of that pricing method, and statistical correlation yielded a high coefficient. For the two C+I loan groups whose interest rates reportedly were based on the prime rate, both the empirical and the theoretical grounds were less firm than for the overnight-loan group. Their correlation coefficients, while not low, are not sufficiently impressive to overcome the substantive reservations.

Alternate Theories of Bank-Loan Pricing

The Federal Reserve's survey of terms of bank lending to commercial and industrial firms constitutes an invaluable periodic flow of statistical information on the largest source of short-term financing to the corporate community. The usefulness of the STBL data is not impaired, of course, by the fact that one section of the report suffers from flaws, some of which are not easily remedied, that have been described in this and the preceding chapter. Even that section, which records respondents' answers to a multiple-choice questio. n which benchmark they use in setting a loan's interest rate, perform the role of introducing a comparatively-unmentioned newcomer among the theories about what determines the interest rate on bank loans. Our review in Chapters 4 and 5 of the treatment of interest in economic theory and in empirical approaches to the subject had found, consistently, that attention has focused predominantly on the long-term bond in the context of capital investment, and under assumed conditions of general equilibrium in the economy. Among the few writers who have expressed views about short-term bank loans, some have regarded those rates as being determined by demand and supply forces, like the prices of commodities under market conditions of perfect competition. A much smaller number of writers were cited who, indeed, perceived that bank loans are not issued under "free-market" conditions but did not offer an explanation of how, that being the case, their rates are determined.

The initiative of the Federal Reserve's quarterly loan survey, in asking respondents to identify which pricing base (or bases) they employ, represents at least a limited or partial occupation of new territory. It is "new" in the sense that it expresses plainly for the first time the assumption by Fed officials that there are identifiable numerical benchmarks inside or outside the individual bank's walls that are employed, "as-is" or with some adjustment, to set the rate on individual business loans. It is also new in the sense that other writers we had examined earlier, whose doctrines typically were formulated within the framework of perfect competition and a macroeconomic equilibrium---whether of the neoclassical variety or the Keynesian---did not view bank lending or other asset markets as being supplier-dominated. Exceptions to that generalization are a small number of economists who have found it fruitful to analyze commercial banking operations with the aid of findings in the field of *monopolistic competition*. These authors have not been discussed heretofore, and it should be useful, before proceeding further, to summarize at this point the main contributions to which we refer.

The appearance in 1933 of Chamberlin's *Theory of Monopolistic Competition* was recognized by economists as a substantive reformulation, primarily with regard to the assumptions of the analytic models dealing with the individual firm and with the interrelation among firms within a given industry. While it also provides insights into some matters of macroeconomic nature, the theory has mainly served to furnish the optical tools for scrutinizing marketing behavior and processes in the real world, with particular reference to a given industrial sector.[5]   It is neither necessary nor relevant here to describe monopolistic competition theory in its entirety. For present purposes, what is needed is to identify its elements that are pertinent to commercial banking.

A key feature of the new theory is its rejection of the assumption posited in the theory of a perfectly competitive market that all firms in a given market are so numerous and so small that no one of them has the power to wield influence over the price and practices in that market. In the actual world, Chamberlin held, markets are smaller and more segmented (or can be made so by various devices). Firms can acquire "market power" by growing larger; but a firm can also win power by finding ways to differentiate its widget from the widgets sold by other firms. If this can be accomplished, either in fact by technical changes or in image through persuasive advertising, the firm can win customer loyalty. The result of these actions and artifices is that firms grow larger in market power and influence than in actual size. In practice, each firm and each competitor can thus set its price and other terms of sale---within limits, being aware that the rival has comparable weapons at its disposal. These oligopolists are seen as ordinarily following among themselves a regime of live-and-let-live, providing their respective customers with some non-priced services or conveniences that partially compensate for any price excesses they perpetrate, and only occasionally menacing their rivals with a round of "cutthroat competition."

In the latter part of the depression of the 1930s, economists were becoming conscious of some non-competitive aspects in the banking market and were beginning to pick away at the prevailing impression that "banking is a highly competitive enterprise." After the dissemination of the theory of monopolistic competition and its general implications, however, monetary economists as well as those in other branches of economics were quick to investigate its applicability. Chandler's findings were that the banking market exhibits features closely analogous to the non-competitive practices identified in industrial product markets, and that the monopolistic competition theory provides a coherent system of thought that is better able to explain these features than previous doctrine. So far as short-term interest rates are concerned, perhaps the main contribution of monopolistic competition theory lies in its clear corroboration that bank loan rates are indeed set by the supplier. Though Chandler and Hodgman made that clear, and the latter stressed the number and complexity of factors entering into a bank's pricing of a given C+I loan application, their analyses did not eventuate in a specific benchmark or mark-up hypothesis resembling that suggested by the STBL.[6]

The past ten years have produced, however, two different variants of a mark-up theory of bank loan pricing that are interesting to compare with each other and with the Fed STBL version. One result of the mixture of competition with monopolistic power that characterizes the real world is that it permits, or even encourages, individual firms to operate ordinarily at less then their capacity level. For a firm in manufacturing, this means that its variable costs (for materials and wages) per unit of output remain fairly constant over the range of below-capacity operation that it normally maintains, and it can respond to a temporary increase in demand without disturbing the stability of its selling price. Rousseas, building partly on Chamberlin and on Kalecki's theory of mark-up of goods, applies the principle to bank lending. He rightly assumes that a bank staff changes little with fluctuations in output, and that a bank's variable costs therefore consist mainly of its "raw material" input costs---i.e., the interest paid on deposits and other borrowed funds. Moving from a definition of a bank's interest-rate spread as the difference between bank costs and what it charges for its loans, this theory adopts the hypothesis that the spread can be measured roughly by comparing the prime rate and the federal funds rate, "which can be taken as a proxy for the cost of funds." This rough approximation is then apparently adjusted and affected over time by the way in which the bank's asset-liability committee manages the types and maturities of the respective holdings. Rousseas's basic concept seems to remain that of the prime rate being determined by a (modified) mark-up over the federal funds rate.[7] Yet we observed (in Chapter 6, Figures 6.1 and 6.2) that the sensitive, spot-like nature of the fed funds rate exerts less influence than his hypothesis suggests on the quarterly behavior of the somewhat more sluggish prime rate, which, he notes, is "an administered 'price' set by banks supposedly for their best customers."

On the basis of a carefully defined hypothesis and supporting research, Goldberg explored a different possible explanation of the prime rate of interest.[8] After acknowledging that little is known about how the prime business loan rate is determined, he proceeded to examine the possibility that the prime is "an administered price based on a bank's average cost of its currently- and previously-issued, but still outstanding, managed liabilities." The cost concept utilized was not an average of full costs (including administrative overhead) but a weighted average of the contractual interest expense on the institution's "present and past deposit liabilities incurred to finance the business loan portfolio," duly weighted by the amount of those liabilities outstanding. For this purpose, the three-month negotiable CD (certificate of deposit in denominations over $100,000) was taken as constituting a bank's managed liabilities. The prime lending rate was regressed against the large CD rate for the period 1975 through October 1980, and the statistical results appear to be "consistent with the hypothesis that banks price their prime rate on the basis of some average" of the costs of their currently outstanding managed liabilities, a phrase plainly alluding to a mark-up.

In addition, the author of this book presents a variation of his own upon the mark-up theme played by Rousseas and Goldberg (and, to some degree, by the STBL). Having been impressed throughout the course of this research by the cogency of the case for taking adequate account of the circumstances which surround the commercial bank as an intermediary---i.e., as a buyer and seller---I have decided to explore a hypothesis that embraces the elements of mark-up and of cost-of-funds on a more inclusive basis. This version, summarized herewith, was undertaken without commitment and with the anticipation that it might yield results no less imperfect than other theories, and would encounter difficulties of method and interpretation no less problematic. In essence, the plan was to develop a weighted average of the rates banks pay on *all* types of deposit, so that this broad measure of the expenditures made for funds could be compared with the prime rate that largely governs loans made with those funds.

For this purpose, the procedure adopted was to develop a quarterly series on deposit interest rates, using data collected in a Federal Reserve survey (different from the Survey on Terms of Bank Lending) on "selected deposits," which has been conducted monthly since 1983 but was performed quarterly on a usable, fairly consistent basis back to the mid-1960s. The Fed's deposit survey customarily gathers figures on the average interest rate and the dollar volume outstanding of the "selected" deposits which, in the early years, consisted of savings deposits, several maturities of low-denomination time deposits, and small amounts of large-size time deposits.[9] Fortunately for present purposes, the quarterly deposit survey applied to the last Wednesday of January, April, July, and October, and we continued to employ those dates during the period after the survey became monthly in late 1983. Since in the last fifteen years the loan survey data are gathered for the first week in February, May, August, and November, the timing dates of the two surveys thus fall within a few days of each other. For constructing the series on the prime rate, we ascertained that national prime rate that was in effect in the survey week of each quarterly loan survey. The series thus described are plotted together in Figure 7.1.

The chart reveals some elements of the general behavior of these curves that are interesting to observe. For instance, with regard to turning points in the business cycle, the prime rate shows about the same characteristics that we saw in Chapter 5 in the overall weighted-average C+I loan rate, on which the prime rate has such a palpable influence. In the earlier years the prime was sluggish in timing and amplitude of response to turning points, but its sensitivity increased, and after 1972 it became virtually synchronous. Though we have no early data for the average deposit rate, it also conformed generally to the cyclical turns from the early 1970s through the 1980s. Regarding the most recent business cycle peak in July 1990, however, the two curves in Figure 7.1 turned downward a full year earlier. But the movement of these series relative to cyclical turning points is not the subject of inquiry at this moment, which concerns what influence is exerted on the prime lending rate by the average rate banks pay on deposits.

Regression of the prime rate against the weighted-average rate of interest paid by banks on their interest-bearing deposits yielded a correlation coefficient of 0.951 for the years 1967 to 1991 inclusive. An array of the *ratio* of the prime rate to the deposit rate---the measure considered to constitute the usual method of mark-up pricing--- exhibited a considerable amount of variation, the ratio ranging from 1.03 to a high of 1.89. Both of those extremes occurred within the less than three-year period, from mid-1969 to the first quarter of 1972, that showed perhaps the least consistency of movement between the two interest series. An *interim* conclusion must be that neither the empirical sequential behavior of the two variables over time nor the statistical regression for the period is sufficiently impressive. Added

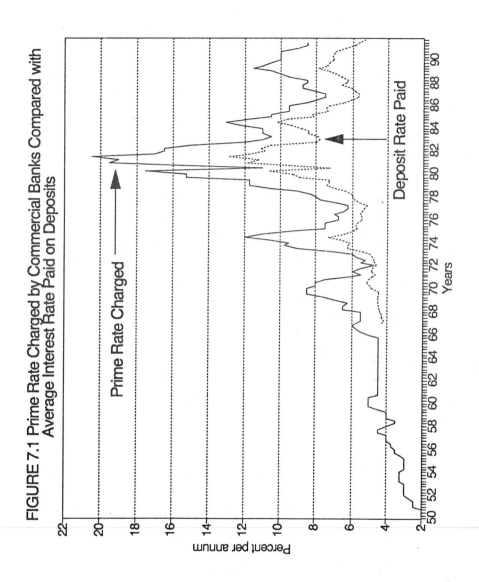

FIGURE 7.1 Prime Rate Charged by Commercial Banks Compared with Average Interest Rate Paid on Deposits

to that observation is a sobering group of economic and institutional reasons for believing that, while the banks' cost of borrowed funds is probably the strongest influence on them in setting their lending rates, this influence was reduced and sometimes overwhelmed by contrary influences during the period measured.

Most of the economic and institutional factors referred to in the previous sentence affect all three of the cost-of-funds hypotheses examined in this section and perhaps also the type of mark-up hypothesis implied in the STBL reports. The closing sections that follow will discuss the factors that complicate or are adverse to the cost-of-funds theory, after first drawing some comparisons *among* them as variant approaches.

Interest Rates and Banks

Having just examined above the main features of three specific experimental approaches to the question of how the interest rates on short-term bank loans to business firms are arrived at, one should make some summary comparisons among them. Thereafter, we can better evaluate the basic concept itself and better identify the factors that favor or hinder demonstrating the validity of the proposition that bank lending rates are mainly influenced by the cost incurred in borrowing funds.

First, as to similarities, the three variant hypotheses share several features in common, either explicitly or by reasonable inference. The rates under scrutiny are those on short-term (less than one year) loans obtained from commercial banks by business borrowers. All three present possible explanations of how a bank's *prime* rate to C+I firms is set; each hypothesis being tested placed its causal assumption in the realm of costs incurred by the bank for its own borrowed funds; but each has selected a different suspect. In addition, all three assume that the prime, however it is established, is used by the bank in some general sense in pricing individual loans, through some sort of mark-up process. It seems implicit that the mark-up is considered as algebraic (can be plus, zero, or minus). Moreover, all three regard bank lending as functioning under conditions of monopolistic competition.

Second, the three approaches differ as to which interest rate on which type of borrowed funds is *mainly* influential in governing the prime rate (probably none of the three would argue strictly in terms of a *sole cause*). Rousseas selects the federal funds rate, with some justification, probably because the interbank loan market is readily accessible for a bank to obtain overnight borrowing and the fed funds rate is sometimes considered as representing a bank's marginal cost of adding an increment of funds. Goldberg or Brown would perhaps doubt that a bank's loan department would wish to consider its prime-rate loans, whose average maturities are 2-4 months, as being governed by the overnight federal funds rate. On this point, in fact, Goldberg stresses the need for matching of maturities between the liabilities and assets in the portfolio. His chosen vehicle as determinant of the prime lending rate is the large-size, 3-month CD, which seems appropriate enough so far as maturity is concerned. Large-size CDs, however, have been more volatile in rate as well as volume than some of the other deposit or certificate accounts. This movement by large CDs might have been even greater if it were not somewhat countered by the fact that their attribute of negotiability gives to the individual holder the option of selling before maturity as well as redemption.

Third, all variants of bank-loan pricing examined here embody a *two-stage* process of mark-up for ostensibly the majority of short-term C+I business loans. That is,

(1)   Variable a, b, or c (depending on which version is considered) plus a mark-up factor yields the prime rate.

(2)   Prime rate plus some algebraic mark-up factor yields the rate on the business customer's loan contract.

The second stage of this dual process includes what is reported (for certain loan types) in the Federal Reserve loan survey's column on loan pricing bases.[10] The first stage is what the three variants of a cost-of-funds hypothesis described in this chapter have presented as possible explanations of the prime rate.

Nevertheless, the theory that short-term bank loans to commercial firms are priced by a mark-up from a prime rate that is determined by the bank's cost of borrowing funds encounters various problems. These arise less in articulating the theory itself than in presenting coherent and convincing empirical evidence to confirm it. The empirical task starts without great difficultly, owing to the existence of the several well-established statistical series previously described on bank deposit rates, lending rates (actual) on business loans, and the nationally posted prime rate. While there have been occasional changes in coverage, definition, and periodicity in the deposit data that render series construction exacting, these obstacles are not insuperable. More basic problems are the following.

      * Ceilings on deposit rates. The Banking Acts of 1933 and 1935 mandated the Federal Reserve to establish and monitor maximum rates of interest that banks could pay on time and savings deposits, and this regime remained in force until late 1980, when new legislation initiated a time-phased dismantling of the ceilings, which proceeded rapidly in the next 3-4 years and ended altogether in early 1986.

After some inaugural adjustment in 1935, the ceilings were not changed during the next two decades; and neither the savings nor time maximum rate exceeded 3 percent until January 1962, when they were fixed at 4 percent. In much of the period up through the 1950s, "the ceiling rates generally were not binding...as banks paid less than the allowed rates."[11] The fact that banks were not always bumping against the rate ceilings and that the maxima were set by fiat rather than by the banks themselves does not, of itself, rule out the possibility that the prime rate was governed to some extent by the banks' controlled cost of funds. Indeed, it seems possible that the virtually horizontal shape of the average interest rate paid on deposits—which did not reach 4.5 percent until late 1968—may have contributed much to the stability of the prime rate in those years.

But if the yoke of maxima-rate limits rested fairly lightly in the late 1950s and the 1960s, the situation was to alter greatly in the next two decades of high economic growth. Interest rates on traditional instruments in the money and capital markets were rising progressively, soon to be joined by the appearance of money market funds and a growth in mutual stock or bond funds that attracted deposits away from banks. This "disintermediation" process put strong pressure on the regulatory bodies to increase the rate ceilings, a delayed reaction procedure that occurred intermittently until the control system was phased out in 1980-1985. The net effect on the nature of bank deposit rates was that for much of the post-war period they were not able to respond freely on the *upward* side to fluctuations in market-determined interest rates; and, at times of such upward pressure, ceiling-controlled deposit interest rates could not be described as being set by the banks themselves.

      * Banks' market power over deposit rates. Professional literature dealing with commercial banking in recent decades has fully recognized the effects on loan interest rates and other aspects of lending operations that derive from the elements of monopolistic competition that characterize the industry. This resulted from

concentrating on competitive relations among banks as sellers and their efforts to develop a degree of market power to attract and hold the continuing loyalty of borrowers through product differentiation. The same incentives that motivate banks as sellers of financial products also inspire their tactics as borrowers, though this fact has been less noticed, probably because banks' promotional activity for deposits was less vigorous in the depression years when the Chamberlin theory was published.[12]

In contrast, this activity has been intense in the past two decades, motivated not only by the robust demand for short-term working capital loans associated with economic expansion but also by the menaced drain of deposits toward mutual funds and other rival instruments. Since the value-added involved in banking is not physically visible, a bank can not advertize the beauty or durability of its loans or the purity or elegance of its deposit certificates. Efforts to differentiate its deposit accounts or certificates from those of rivals are confined to offering fractional variations in the rate itself, the compounding of interest, and other items; and to asserting boldly the solidity of the bank, its friendliness, etc. The relevance of these activities to the theory of lending-rate determination is that (1) banks engage in monopolistic behavior toward depositors as well as monopsonistic behavior toward borrowers and rivals; (2) the targets of these efforts are *all types* of present and potential depositors or certificate holders, and thus the negotiable large CDs are not the only sort of "managed liabilities;" (3) the degree to which the bank succeeds in holding depositors, and at what terms, affects the lending rates on its loans, and profitability.

　　*　Attribution of borrowed funds to specific bank assets. Hypotheses about what determines the banks' prime rate on business loans, including the three theories reviewed in this chapter, sometimes postulate that the prime is mainly, if not wholly, governed by a cost incurred by banks in the performance of their function as intermediaries. And the power of example or symmetry suggests that this cost be measured by a rate of interest that the banks themselves have paid. Two versions of the cost-of-funds proposition, in following that train of thought, assigned the governing role to a single average rate---the federal funds in one case and the large negotiable CD rate in the other case---for certain specified reasons. The third variant assigned the role to the weighted average of all rates paid by banks on their interest-bearing deposits, principally for the reason that the deposits that banks acquire form the major portion of total bank resources of loanable funds and are commingled with the others. It

seemed dubious to assume that monies placed in one type of deposit account would necessarily be earmarked for use in only one or a few types of business loan.

While the author's use of a weighted composite of deposit rates paid is probably an improved version of the cost-of-funds thesis regarding the prime rate, it does not suffice for the still-larger aspects of the attribution problem. The prime rate on business loans is still surrounded with a degree of mystery, not only respecting its determination at a given moment and its movement over time but also the manner in which it is adjusted up or down in individual loan operations. What is generally uncontested, however, is that its habitat and its major influence are in the category of short-term commercial and industrial loans. That instrument remains the distinctive, identifying loan category of the commercial bank, and is statistically chronicled by a quarterly loan survey. Other loan categories have their own different customers, purposes, loan terms, risks, repayment records. How much of the impact from movements in the cost of paying interest on the deposits of a bank (or the banking system) can be assumed to affect the business loan department, as compared with other loan operations, is hard to demonstrate. Movements in bank costs on deposits can also affect the institution's decisions about investment in securities as well in loans.

The reader will perceive that the Federal Reserve's survey of business loan terms does not confront the attribution problem just discussed, owing to the fact that the STBL's perception of the process of mark-up pricing does not involve a bank's cost of funds. If the author is interpreting the STBL's finding correctly, they hold that short-term loan rates are indeed governed by reference to, or taking account of, some known interest rate; and that specifically the loans are priced by reference (a) to the prime rate or (b) to some domestic or foreign market rate that is extra-mural to the bank and not, or not necessarily, a cost incurred by the bank. This inference may be incorrect, since it is not drawn from any formal statement but from the facts that the STBL report form makes no provision for indicating a cost of funds to the bank as being used for loan pricing, and that informal Fed discussions stress a view that banks' lending terms are governed by current market rates rather than bank expenditures.

Concluding Observations

As this study has progressed, we have discerned the tenacious habit of economic theorists and practitioners to regard the subject of interest and interest rates as significant only with regard to the theory of long-term capital formation. Increasingly, however, there has developed a greater awareness of the role of short-term lending and borrowing operations and the relevance that this bank financing of working-capital requirements bears to the general level of economic activity and to other institutions in the financial markets. As with any entity or transaction that comes under scrutiny in a money economy, the question soon arises as to price determination. So long as economic analysis remained committed to a system of thought centered on a hypothetical economy in a state of equilibrium, whose firms and industries performed under conditions of perfect, or pure, competition, it was difficult to fit activity in a field like banking into that static framework. It tended to be ignored.

Contemporary economics has, perhaps unwittingly, tended to move in two parallel and simultaneous directions---one being to study the *creation* of an interest rate or other price under more realistic assumptions, and the other being to study the internal or exogenous forces that shape how it *evolves*. Both approaches are productive. The latter method is necessary in the private sector for analyzing current market developments and for corporate planning; and for researchers it is fruitful as an exercise, if not in dynamics, in successive statics.

Continued attention is equally needed to the subject of the "determination" or birthing of an interest rate, a phenomenon which is not sufficiently understood and accepted. A better perception of this process could, in particular, be useful to economic policy makers in detecting structural changes or abrupt institutional shifts, their implications, and any need for governmental or central-bank action.

So far as choosing or evaluating any *specific* determination theory is concerned, our examination of the hypothesis that interest rates on business loans are set by a mark-up from some cost or costs incurred by the lending banks produces qualified results. Each of the three candidates for the role of bank cost employed as base for the *first step* of the mark-up process (i.e., the step applying a ratio to bank cost to set the prime rate) made a showing that was less than satisfying from an empirical standpoint, and some of them are not sufficiently cogent theoretically. The task of demonstrating any theory in this field confronts a thorny path. "The best that we can expect is to show that the facts as we find them are not inconsistent with the theory maintained."[13]

Two of the obstacles confronting the theory should be mentioned. One stems from the maintenance over the period 1935 into the mid-

1980s of a regime of maximum limits on deposit interest rates, which not only controlled those rates but produced effects on the relationship between deposit costs and lending rates that varies in nature, depending on other concomitant economic factors. That fact stands, though one can not be completely censorious of the ceilings when one recalls the restrictive practices that had prevailed before them.[14] Another risk to beware of is that if the cost-of-funds thesis is propounded in too doctrinaire and unqualified a fashion it could give the impression that the state of demand is completely ignored by banks in their pricing, which would overstate the facts. A bank can vary the *size* of the mark-up amount---in either step of the two-step process---according to the strength of loan demand or other current market circumstances.

Indeed, over the period 1967-1991 the variations in ratio of the prime rate to the weighted-average deposit rate show some rough relation to cyclical turning points, the ratio tending to rise slightly toward and immediately after a peak, and to decline at and often 1-2 quarters after a trough. In addition, one finding emerging from Chapter 5---perhaps the principal one---concerns the relationship of the growth of GNP to the weighted-average interest rate on short-term C+I loans, i.e., to the average rate charged to business borrowers that results from the banks' mark-up from the prime rate and other pricing bases. We found that *movements* in the average interest rate on new business loans frequently were strongly influenced by the rate of growth in GNP. That is, high *rates of increase* (over the preceding year) in the country's aggregate value of output and income (in current dollars) were often accompanied or quickly followed by a rise in the terms and volume of the short-term bank instruments that constitute an important source of financing those fluctuations of national product and income. Despite the clear functional association, the lending rate's statistical relationship to GNP growth rates certainly is not uniform in timing and amplitude.

Only six years have passed since ceiling limits on bank deposit rates were fully terminated in the aftermath of an assortment of other major dislocations in the U.S. economy associated with large shifts in relative prices of petroleum and other commodities, disequilibrium in the balance of international payments, and large and chronic deficits in the federal budget that had pro-cyclical economic effects. The economy requires a longer period that is free of mandatory ceilings on deposit rates before one can adequately judge the effects on those rates and especially the effects on their level relative to other banking variables and the economy at large. In the meantime, given the presence of administered pricing and management of both loans and deposits in the banking industry and given the elements of monopolistic competition that permeate the modern "price-tag economy" in general, a theory that regards bank lending rates of interest as governed largely by the bank's cost of borrowed funds, while they remain subject to being *influenced* by significant movements in the growth of nominal GNP, seems superior to other explanations.

Arresting implications follow from this finding, if it is correct, for consideration by the central bank in shaping its monetary policies. At the end of December 1973, the *interest-bearing* deposits at U.S. insured commercial banks amounted to 54.6 percent of their total deposits. By end 1983, that share had risen to 74.9 percent and at the end of 1991 constituted over 81 percent of total deposits. During that period of the 1980s, characterized by changeful innovations in financial practices and by more permissive banking legislation and supervision, bank deposits had also changed in other ways---becoming more liquid and transferable, but less covered by minimum reserve requirements.[15] Given those developments, if the interest rates paid on the banks' deposit liabilities do indeed largely govern the rates banks set on their loans to business firms, the behavior of lending rates will continue, perhaps increasingly, to depend on the course taken by the interest rates and other provisions applying to deposits.

Notes

1. Fisher 1930, pp. 487-492, 374-386. He was equally adept at formulating hypotheses about interest or price determination under rigid abstractions and at observing dynamic developments under actual conditions.

2. Lutz 1968, pp. 277-278; and Ohlin 1937, p. 424.

3. With reference to his own and other studies, Coutts describes the practices of manufacturers and other non-bank firms in setting their selling prices in reference to various concepts of unit cost. Coutts 1987, pp. 158-159. Okun 1981 analyzes "customer markets" for both goods, pp. 138-154, and financial assets, pp. 192-198.

4. Alhadeff 1967; Chamberlin 1933; Chandler 1938; Rousseas 1986.

5. More than twenty years after publishing the *Theory*, Chamberlin noted, "It is perhaps only natural that the theory should be associated primarily with the field of industry, where examples of 'differentiated' products, of oligopoly, of selling costs, etc. seem to abound...Even in the monetary area it has been shown that the typical banker sells a differentiated service and that oligopoly power is very general." Chamberlin 1957, pp. 5-7. In the second sentence of this quotation, Chamberlin probably was referring to Chandler's analysis. His own 1933 *Theory* did not address banking; nor did his 1957 book mention the banking market, save for the one sentence just quoted.

6. Chandler 1938, pp. 1-22. Hodgman's survey of the criteria employed in pricing loans at the moment of their origination was supported by perhaps equal attention to the "process by which the prime rate of interest is raised or lowered", which he identified as "the informal one of price leadership...by informal concerted action on the part of the principal banks." Hodgman 1963, pp. 120-122.

7. Rousseas 1986, pp. 50-61. His hypothesis about rate determination is accompanied by observations on recent factual and policy developments.

8. Goldberg 1982, pp. 277-295. The quotations in this paragraph are from pp. 278, 281, and 292 respectively.

9. The term "selected deposits" signifies only that certain minor or specialized types of time deposits, such as Christmas Club accounts and noninterest-bearing holdings, are omitted, as are demand deposits. Thus the coverage, which included new types of certificate and checkable accounts as they were "innovated" in the late 1970s and 1980s, is suitable to present purposes. Prior to 1967, a deposit survey was conducted only infrequently and at irregular intervals, and it covered only banks that were members of the Federal Reserve System. Note that in the deposit series the interest rates are weighted by the volume of the respective deposits outstanding, whereas in the C+I loan series the rates are weighted by the amount of new loans of the respective maturity groups made during the survey week.

10. Cf. also Goldberg's statement the even "non-prime rates are typically set by tying them formally or informally to the prime." Goldberg 1982, p. 277.

11. Mahoney et al. 1987, p. 21. Regarding the deregulation transition, this paper said, "Judging by the movements of deposit offering rates, banks and thrift institutions did not tie these rates directly to market yields...Removal of the ceilings...on the six-month account resulted in considerable diversity...it appears that the interest rate ceilings on this account were holding many deposit rates above, rather than below, freely competitive rates." Pp. 8-9. See also Fellner 1976, pp. 106-107.

12. See Chandler 1938, pp. 1-22, in which the analysis is supported by documented accounts of monopolistic elements in banking from the nineteenth as well as the twentieth century. Also Alhadeff 1967.

13. Fisher 1930, p. 372.

14. In addition to the ways in which an individual bank seeks to distinguish its own lending and deposit facilities from others, actions are taken by groups of banks and by clearing-houses and trade associations to restrict competition in the interest of "interbank cooperation." Cf. Chandler 1938, pp. 10-16.

15. Regarding these changes, see Brown 1987, chapters 2 and 3; and Rousseas 1986, pp. 54-61.

Sources for Tables and Figures

Some of the tables and figures in this book do not specify the source of the data presented therein. The purpose of those omissions is to devote as much space as possible to portraying the data, given the limited dimensions of the printed page. Although the author has been careful to describe the nature and sources of the data in the surrounding text, the list below assembles the origins for tables and charts concerned. All the tables were created by selecting and statistically manipulating the pertinent numbers from published materials, and in no case was a previously published table used in its original form. In all instances but one the tables and figures draw upon statistical series and related data appearing in documents that are in the public domain. (In that one case, the source and the permission to use are stated in the Notes to Chapter 5.) As mentioned in the Preface, many of the numbers used come from the voluminous data gathered by the Federal Reserve Board of Governors. In the list below, the monthly *Federal Reserve Bulletin* published by the Board of Governors is referred to here as *F.R. Bulletin*.

Tables

2.1   Statistical Release E.2 and *F.R. Bulletin*.

5.1   Calculated from series in *F.R. Bulletin* and *Annual Statistical Digest* for pertinent years.

5.3   Calculated from GNP series in *Annual Report of Council of Economic Advisors* for 1991; and average C+I interest figures presented earlier in this book.

Figures

2.1   Weighted-average interest rates on new C+I bank loans, as reported in quarterly Survey of Terms of Bank Lending made by Federal Reserve.

3.1   *F.R. Bulletin* tables of amounts outstanding of bank C+I loans and of nonfinancial firm borrowings in commercial paper market.

3.2   Weighted-average C+I interest rates taken from preceding tables and volume of those loans outstanding: in actual current dollars, and in constant dollars. Calculated from *F.R. Bulletin* tables.

5.1   *F.R. Bulletin* and releases.

5.2   *F.R. Bulletin* series on new corporate bonds issued and on market yield, by grade of bond.

5.3   Consumer price changes and changes in GNP price deflator from Department of Commerce and *Annual Report of Council of Economic Advisers* (CEA).

5.4   Same as 5.3.

5.5   Calculated from Commerce and CEA series on annual change in GNP.

5.6   (a) Same as 5.5; (b) calculation of annual *change* in the weighted-average C+I interest used throughout this book.

5.7   Calculated from data used in Figures 5.1–5.6.

5.8   Graphical presentation of the Gorman data, as described in Notes 16 and 17 of Chapter 5.

5.9   Data from Figure 5.8 on profits, compared with usual interest-rate average on short-term bank loans to C+I firms.

6.1   Table in *F.R. Bulletin* and in Fed's *Annual Statistical Digest* shows prime rate on business loans prevailing nationally at commercial banks, noting date of any rate change. Figure 6.1 plots the prime rate in effect at the time of each quarterly STBL survey date, together with the weighted-average rate on new loans reported for that survey.

6.2   The usual weighted-average C+I interest rate just mentioned is shown with the *F.R. Bulletin* figure on the average rate prevailing, on that survey period, for "federal funds" in the inter-bank loan market.

7.1   The series on the national prime lending rate (see 6.1 above) is shown here. The other curve is a series calculated by the author, a weighted-average of the several different interest rates that banks paid to depositors. This new series on deposit-rates paid by banks has not been published previously.

Bibliography

Alhadeff, David A. 1967. "Monopolistic Competition and Banking Markets," in Robert E. Kuenne, ed., *Monopolistic Competition Theory: Studies in Impact,* pp. 357–378. New York: John Wiley & Sons.

Aristotle. Date unknown. *Politics.* Benjamin Jowett translation 1945. Oxford: Clarendon Press.

Board of Governors. 1976. *Banking and Monetary Statistics, 1941–1970.* Washington: Board of Governors of the Federal Reserve System.

_____. 1981. *Annual Statistical Digest 1970–1979.* Washington: Board of Governors of the Federal Reserve System.

_____. 1984. *The Federal Reserve System: Purposes and Functions,* 7th ed. Washington: Board of Governors of the Federal Reserve System.

_____. 1984a. "Announcements: Monetary and Credit Actions." *Federal Reserve Bulletin,* April 1980, pp. 314–315.

Brady, Thomas F. 1985. "Changes in Loan Pricing and Business Lending at Commercial Banks." *Federal Reserve Bulletin,* January 1985, pp. 1–13.

Brown, Weir M. 1987. *Keeping the Central Bank Central: U.S. Monetary Policy and the Banking System.* Boulder: Westview Press.

Buchanan, James M. 1969. *Cost and Choice.* Chicago: Markham Publishing Co.

_____. 1987. "Opportunity Cost," in John Eatwell et al., eds., *The New Palgrave: A Dictionary of Economics,* Vol. 3, pp. 718–721. London: Macmillan Press Ltd.

Buchanan, Susan, and Seymour Gaylinn, eds. 1987. *1987 CRB Commodity Yearbook.* New York: Commodity Research Bureau.

Burns, Arthur F. 1987. *The Ongoing Revolution in American Banking.* Posthumous. Mark Perlman and Arthur L. Broida, eds. Washington: American Enterprise Institute for Public Policy Research.

Cagan, Phillip. 1972. *The Channels of Monetary Effects on Interest Rates.* New York: National Bureau of Economic Research.

_____, and Robert E. Lipsey. 1978. *The Financial Effects of Inflation.* NBER General Series No. 103. Cambridge: Ballinger Publishing Co.

Cargill, Thomas F., and Gillian G. Garcia. 1985. *Financial Reform in the 1980s.* Stanford: Hoover Institution Press.

Chamberlin, Edward H. 1933. *The Theory of Monopolistic Competition.* Cambridge: Harvard University Press.

_____. 1957. *Towards a More General Theory of Value.* New York: Oxford University Press.

Chandler, Lester V. 1938. "Monopolistic Elements in Commercial Banking." *Journal of Political Economy,* Vol. XLVI (1938), pp. 1–22.

_____ . 1970. "Impacts of Theory on Policy: The Early Years of the Federal Reserve," in David P. Eastburn, ed., *Men, Money, and Policy*, pp. 41–53. Philadelphia: Federal Reserve Bank of Philadelphia.

Code of Federal Regulations 1992. *CFR Title 12, Banks and Banking.* Part 225, Sec. 145. Washington: Office of the Federal Register, National Archives and Records Administration.

Conard, Joseph W. 1966. *The Behavior of Interest Rates.* New York: National Bureau of Economic Research.

Cook, Timothy Q., and Timothy D. Rowe. 1986. *Instruments of the Money Market.* 6th ed. Richmond: Federal Reserve Bank of Richmond.

Council of Economic Advisers. 1991. *The Annual Report of the Council of Economic Advisers.* Washington: U.S. Government Printing Office.

Coutts, K. J. 1987. "Average Cost Pricing," in John Eatwell et al., eds., *The New Palgrave: A Dictionary of Economics*, Vol. 1, pp. 158–159.

Davenport, Herbert J. 1913. *The Economics of Enterprise.* 1943 ed. New York: Macmillan Co.

Estrella, Arturo. 1986. "Domestic Banks and Their Competitors in the Prime Commercial Loan Market," in Richard G. Davis, ed., *Recent Trends in Commercial Bank Profitability: A Staff Study*, pp. 159–177. New York: Federal Reserve Bank of New York.

Fellner, William. 1976. *Towards a Reconstruction of Macroeconomics: Problems of Theory and Policy.* Washington: American Enterprise Institute for Public Policy Research.

Fischer, Gerald C. 1982. *The Prime: Myth and Reality.* Philadelphia: Temple University.

Fisher, Irving. 1896. *Appreciation and Interest.* Reprint of 1925. New York: Augustus M. Kelley.

_____ . 1930. *The Theory of Interest.* New York: Macmillan Co.

Fleming, J. Marcus. 1978. *Essays on Economic Policy.* New York: Columbia Press.

Goldberg, Michael A. 1982. "The Pricing of the Prime Rate."*Journal of Banking and Finance*, Vol. 6, June 1982, pp. 277–296.

Goldenweiser, E. A. 1951. *American Monetary Policy.* New York: McGraw-Hill Book Co.

Goodfriend, Marvin, and William Whelpley. 1986. "Federal Funds," in Timothy Q. Cook and Timothy D. Rowe, eds. *Instruments of the Money Market*, 6th ed. Richmond: Federal Reserve Bank of Richmond.

Guttentag, Jack M., ed. 1971. *Essays on Interest Rates, Vol. II.* NBER General Series No. 93. New York: National Bureau of Economic Research.

Harrod, Roy F. 1969. *Money.* London: Macmillan.

_____ . 1973. *Economic Dynamics.* London: Macmillan.

Hawtrey, R. G. 1937. Rejoinder III to "Alternative Theories of the Rate of Interest." *Economic Journal*, September 1937, pp. 436–443.

_____ . 1937a. *Capital and Employment.* London: Longmans, Green and Co.

Hodgman, Donald R. 1963. *Commercial Bank Loan and Investment Policy.* Champaign: Bureau of Economic and Business Research, University of Illinois.

Kaufman, George G. 1973. *Money, the Financial System, and the Economy.* Chicago: Rand McNally & Co.

Kettl, Donald F. 1986. *Leadership at the Fed*. New Haven: Yale University Press.

Keynes, John Maynard, 1936. *The General Theory of Employment, Interest, and Money*. New York: Harcourt, Brace Co.

_____. 1937. "Alternative Theories of the Rate of Interest." *Economic Journal*, June 1937, pp. 241–252.

Koyck, L. M., and Maria J. 'T Hooft-Welvaars. 1965. "Economic Growth, Marginal Productivity of Capital, and the Rate of Interest," in F. H. Hahn and F.P.R. Brechling, eds., *The Theory of Interest Rates*. London: Macmillan & Co.

Laub, P. Michael. 1988. "Commercial Loan Securitization." Unpublished paper written for American Bankers Association, March 25, 1988. (Used with permission of author.)

Litan, Robert E. 1987. *What Should Banks Do?* Washington: The Brookings Institution.

Lutz, Friedrich A. 1968. *The Theory of Interest*. Dordrecht: D. Reidel Publishing Co.

Mahoney, Patrick I., and Mary M. McLaughlin, Paul F. O'Brien, and Alice P. White. 1987. *Responses to Deregulation: Retail Deposit Pricing from 1983 Through 1985*. Staff Study 151. Washington: Board of Governors of Federal Reserve System.

Mayer, Thomas, James S. Duesenberry, and Robert Z. Aliber. 1981. *Money, Banking, and the Economy*. New York: W. W. Norton & Co.

McLaughlin, Mary M., and Martin H. Wolfson. 1988. "The Profitability of Insured Commercial Banks in 1987." *Federal Reserve Bulletin*, July 1988, pp. 403–418.

Meek, Paul. 1982. *U.S. Monetary Policy and Financial Markets*. New York: Federal Reserve Bank of New York.

Melton, William C. 1985. *Inside the Fed: Making Monetary Policy*. Homewood (Ill.): Dow Jones-Irwin.

Meltzer, Allan H. 1988. *Keynes's Monetary Theory: A Different Interpretation*. Cambridge: Cambridge University Press.

Meulendyke, Ann-Marie. 1989. *U.S. Monetary Policy and Financial Markets*. New York: Federal Reserve Bank of New York.

Mill, John Stuart. 1848. *Principles of Political Economy*. 7th ed. 1971. London: Longmans, Green and Co.

Ohlin, Bertil. 1936. "Introduction," in Knut Wicksell's *Interest and Prices*, English ed. 1936. (See Wicksell 1898.)

_____. 1937. Rejoinder I to "Alternative Theories of the Rate of Interest." *Economic Journal*, September 1937, pp. 423–427.

Okun, Arthur M. 1981. *Prices and Quantities: A Macroeconomic Analysis*. Posthumous. Washington: The Brookings Institution.

Panico, Carlo. 1987. "Interest and Profit," in John Eatwell et al., eds., *The New Palgrave: A Dictionary of Economics*, Vol. 2, pp. 877–879. London: Macmillan Press Ltd.

Patinkin, Don. 1965. *Money, Interest, and Prices*. 2nd ed. New York: Harper & Row.

Pavel, Christine. 1986. "Securitization." *Economic Perspectives* (Federal Reserve Bank of Chicago), July/August 1986, pp. 16–31.

_____, and David Phillis. 1987. "Why Commercial Banks Sell Loans: An Empirical Analysis." *Economic Perspectives*, May/June 1987, pp. 3–14.

Pearce, David W., ed. 1986. *The MIT Dictionary of Modern Economics*. Cambridge: The MIT Press.

Polakoff, Murray E., and Morris Budin. 1973. *The Prime Rate: A Study.* Chicago: Association of Reserve City Bankers.

Ricardo, David. 1811. *The High Price of Bullion.* Gonner ed. 1923. London: G. Bell and Sons, Ltd.

———. 1821. *Principles of Political Economy and Taxation.* Gonner ed. 1903. London: G. Bell and Sons, Ltd.

Robbins, Lionel C. 1970. *The Evolution of Modern Economic Thought.* Chicago: Aldine Publishing Co.

Robertson, D. H. 1937. Rejoinder II to "Alternative Theories of the Rate of Interest." *Economic Journal,* September 1937, pp. 428–436.

———. 1953. "More Notes on the Rate of Interest." *Review of Economic Studies,* Vol. 21 (1953–1954), pp. 136–141.

———. 1959. *Lectures on Economic Principles, Vol. III,* pp. 77–92.

Roll, Eric. 1974. *A History of Economic Thought.* 4th ed. Homewood (Ill.): Richard D. Irwin, Inc.

Roosa, Robert V. 1951. "Interest Rates and the Central Bank," in *Money, Trade, and Economic Growth.* New York: Macmillan.

———. 1956. *Federal Reserve Operations in the Money and Government Securities Markets.* New York: Federal Reserve Bank of New York.

Rousseas, Stephen. 1986. *Post Keynesian Monetary Economics.* Armonk (N.Y.): M. E. Sharpe, Inc.

Shackle, G.L.S. 1961. "Recent Theories Concerning the Nature and Role of Interest." *Economic Journal,* June 1961, pp. 209–254.

Solow, Robert M. 1991. *The Rate of Return and the Rate of Interest.* Stockholm: Industrial Institute for Economic and Social Research.

Spiegel, Henry W. 1983. *The Growth of Economic Thought.* 2nd ed. Durham: Duke University Press.

———. 1987. "Usury," in John Eatwell et al., eds., *The New Palgrave: A Dictionary of Economics,* Vol. 4, pp. 769–770. London: Macmillan Press, Ltd.

Summers, Lawrence H. 1983. "The Nonadjustment of Nominal Interest Rates," in James Tobin, ed., *Macroeconomics, Prices, and Quantities.* Washington: The Brookings Institution, pp. 201–203.

Tanzi, Vito. 1984. *Taxation, Inflation, and Interest Rates.* Washington: International Monetary Fund.

Thomson, Dorothy Lampen. 1973. *Adam Smith's Daughters.* Jericho (N.Y.): Exposition Press.

Thorn, Richard S., ed. 1976. *Monetary Theory and Policy.* New York: Praeger Publishers.

Thornton, Henry. 1802. *An Enquiry into the Nature and Effects of the Paper Credit of Great Britain.* Von Hayek ed. 1939. New York: Farrar & Rinehart.

United States Code Service. 1984. *12 USCS, Banks and Banking.* Chapter 17, Section 1841, p. 341. Rochester: Laywers Co-operative Publishing Co.

U.S. Congress. House Committee on Banking, Finance, and Urban Affairs. 1981. Robert D. Auerbach, ed. *Staff Report on the Prime Rate,* April 1981. Washington: Bureau of Engraving and Printing.

Usher, Abbott Payson. 1943. *The Early History of Deposit Banking in Mediterranean Europe.* Cambridge: Harvard University Press.

Van Horne, James C. 1978. *Financial Market Rates and Flows.* Englewood Cliffs (N.J.): Prentice-Hall.

Wicksell, Knut. 1898. *Interest and Prices.* English ed. 1936. London: Macmillan and Co.

_____. 1906. *Lectures on Political Economy.* 2 vols. English translation 1935. London: George Routledge & Sons, Ltd.

Wilcox, James A. 1990. "Nominal Interest-Rate Effects on Real Consumer Expenditure." *Business Economics,* Vol. XXV, October 1990, pp. 31–36.

Wojnilower, Albert M., and Richard E. Speagle. 1962. "The Prime Rate—Part 2." *Monthly Review* (Federal Reserve Bank of New York), May 1962, pp. 70–73.

Young, Ralph A. 1973. *Instruments of Monetary Policy: The Role of the Federal Reserve System.* Washington: International Monetary Fund.